jams, conserves
and preserving

Contents

Notes

Standard level spoon measurements are used in all recipes.
1 tablespoon = one 15 ml spoon
1 teaspoon = one 5 ml spoon

Both metric and imperial measurements have been given in all recipes. Use one set of measurements only and not a mixture of both.

Milk should be full fat unless otherwise stated.

Fresh herbs should be used unless otherwise stated. If unavailable, use dried herbs as an alternative but halve the quantities stated.

Ovens should be pre-heated to the specified temperature – if using a fan-assisted oven, follow manufacturer's instructions for adjusting the time and the temperature.

Pepper should be freshly ground black pepper unless otherwise stated.

Nuts and nut derivatives
This book includes dishes made with nuts and nut derivatives. It is advisable for readers with known allergic reactions to nuts and nut derivatives and those who may be potentially vulnerable to these allergies, such as pregnant and nursing mothers, invalids, the elderly, babies and children, to avoid dishes made with nuts and nut oils. It is also prudent to check the labels of pre-prepared ingredients for the possible inclusion of nut derivatives.

Vegetarians should look for the 'V' symbol on a cheese to ensure it is made with vegetarian rennet. There are vegetarian forms of Parmesan, Feta, Cheddar, Cheshire, Red Leicester, dolcelatte and many goats' cheeses, among others.

Preserving jars should be sterilized before use. Some fruits and vegetables need to be blanched before sterilization.

jams, conserves and preserving

photography by Akiko Ida

HACHETTE illustrated

If you turn your garden produce into preserves, you will have the pleasure of eating healthy, natural fruits and vegetables all year round, in and out of season. Making preserves is easy. Here are all the tips you need to be successful.

It is very easy to preserve fruit and vegetables at home. Anyone – even beginners – can achieve great results, but you do need to be fussy about quality. Only really good-quality fruits and vegetables make good preserves.

If you are lucky enough to have fruit trees or a vegetable garden, the best time to pick the produce is in the early morning, before the sun gets hot, but wait until the dew has evaporated. Avoid picking fruit and vegetables in wet weather. It is best to harvest fruits and vegetables early in the season, when they are just ripe.

For successful preserves, you must follow strict food safety rules. Use only proper preserving jars, with rubber seals and metal clips or screw-tops. You can use the jars over and over again, but you must use a brand-new rubber seal each time.

There are two ways to sterilize the jars after filling: you can boil them or use a pressure-cooker.

Be careful

With certain dishes
For preserving fish, poultry or meat, and for some vegetables with a low acidity, you are strongly recommended to use a pressure cooker. A high temperature – above the normal boiling point of water at 100°C (212°F) – is required to kill bacteria and to prevent the growth of moulds, yeasts, etc. Obviously, this is not possible using a simple saucepan.

When preserves go off
If the cover of a preserving jar has 'blown' – that is, bulges – if it opens too easily, if the rubber seal has become distended, or if you discover mould in the jar, don't take risks. Throw the preserve away.

Sterilization

Blanching fruits and vegetables
Some fruits and vegetables need to be blanched as well as washed before they are sterilized. Blanching helps retain their colour and prevents them from becoming too acid. Don't forget to rinse fruit and vegetables after blanching. And you should never re-use the blanching water for cooking the produce.

Sterilizing jars
Before using preserving jars, you should wash and dry them. Then place them in a pan of boiling water for several minutes in order to sterilize them. Stand the jars upside down to drain on a clean tea towel. You may also sterilize them in your oven at 110°C (225°F), Gas Mark ¼ for 5 minutes.

Bottling
When filling jars, do not press down on the fruit or vegetables. When adding liquid, never fill the jar completely. Leave a headspace of at least 1.5 cm (¾ inch), so that the rubber seal does not burst or distort during sterilization.

Sealing
Once you have filled the jar, don't forget to fit a brand-new rubber seal. The seal is designed to keep air out of the jar.

Sterilizing the preserves
To minimize disturbance to the jar during sterilization, wrap it in a towel after ensuring the seal is airtight. Place the jar in a large saucepan or pressure cooker. Add water to cover. If using a pressure cooker, reduce the time given in the recipe by one-third. If you do not have a pressure cooker, a large saucepan will do, provided it is sufficiently deep to prevent it from boiling over. Pay careful attention to correct temperatures and cooking times. Always wait for the water to come to the boil before you start to count the sterilization time. Once the correct time has elapsed, turn off the heat and leave the jars to cool in the pressure cooker or saucepan.

Storage
Store in a cool, dry place away from light. It is sensible to label the jars with their contents and the date.

Use by ...

How long will it keep?
It all depends on the preserving method.

Plain

Vegetables that have been bottled in water or small preserves may keep for a whole year, but if you notice mould form on the top, don't hesitate to throw it away. Either the seal wasn't airtight or the sterilization wasn't long enough.

In salt or vinegar

Preserves using salt or vinegar, such as capers, pickles and chutneys, are normally consumed within a month or two, but can keep for a very long time – even more than a year. However, some vegetables, such as pickled beetroot, and certain fish, such as salted anchovies, keep for only about 3 months. It is important, therefore, to label your preserves with dates.

In oil

Preserves using oil, like those in salt or vinegar, are normally consumed within a month or two of making. On the other hand, they can be stored for 10–12 months.

With added sugar

Preserves that use sugar, like jams and jellies, will keep very well for a long time. Syrups, such as lemon or mint, however, have to be consumed more or less straight away, as they will not keep for more than a month.

In alcohol

Preserves bottled in alcohol are the ones that keep longest. In fact, the longer the fruits macerate in the alcohol, the more tender they will be. You will need to wait at least 2 months after bottling before you open the jar.

Drying

Herbs, vegetables, such as mushrooms, and fruits that have been dried will keep for 6–8 months. Make sure that the fruits have thoroughly dried out and that none of them has rotted or contaminated the others. Finally, be sure to keep them in a perfectly dry place.

Making mango chutney

• To prepare a mango, cut it in half near the pit and slice into the flesh of the first half making a criss-cross pattern to produce cubes, press the skin underneath to separate the cubes, then cut the flesh from the skin. Repeat with the other half of the mango.

• Place the cubes in a dish, add brown sugar, vinegar and spices and leave to macerate.

• Cook the mango with the sugar and spices over a very low heat.
The mixture will gradually thicken as you stir.

• Ladle the chutney into a sterilized preserving jar and seal with an airtight lid, not forgetting to use a new rubber seal.

• Turn the jar upside down to produce a vacuum.

• Store the chutney for at least 15 days before eating. It will keep for a long time if stored unopened in a dark, dry place.
Serve as an accompaniment to rice, fish and white meat.
(See also detailed recipe page 62.)

How it works

This is basically a book for lovers of good food. The recipes that follow are easy to make, but it won't do any harm just to recall why particular techniques of conservation are considered suitable for some foods and not others. These techniques can be categorized as follows: coating, dehydration, the use of preservatives and sterilization.

Coating

Coating with fats, such as oil or duck fat, protects foods from the air. They are therefore prevented from oxidizing too quickly and becoming mouldy. The fat coating also retains the moisture in the food. Because the food does not dry out, it looks better longer.

Dehydration

The drying process removes all the moisture from fruits and vegetables to stop them from going bad. They can be dried naturally in the sun, placed in an oven with the door left ajar or dried over a stove.

Using preservatives

Preserving in salt, alcohol, vinegar, or sugar halts the development of microbes.
Make sure that you use the right type of product: sea salt is better than mineral salt; vinegar should be strong (7%); spirits are best if between 48% and 52%; use refined sugar, such as preserving, granulated or caster. Avoid brown sugar, icing sugar or demerara, even if these are what you normally prefer.

Sterilization

Plain preserves always need to be sterilized. Use boiling water or a pressure cooker. The heat drives the air from the jars, thereby preventing moulds from developing.
Sterilization times vary according to whether you use a saucepan or pressure cooker.
The times given in the recipes should be calculated from the moment the water boils.
If you use a pressure cooker, the times indicated should be reduced by one-third.

Bottling...

• Cherries in alcohol

Place the cherries in a sterilized preserving jar and cover them with sugar and eau de vie (colourless brandy), grappa or vodka, to within 1.5–3 cm (¾–1½ inches) of the top. Seal and store in a dark, dry place.
(See also recipe page 142.)

• Dried tomatoes in oil

Place the dried tomatoes in a sterilized preserving jar. Pour in olive oil until the tomatoes are completely covered. Seal and store the jar in a dark, dry place. Once the jar has been opened, keep the tomatoes covered with oil to prevent them from drying out.
(See also recipe page 16.)

• Anchovies in salt

Place anchovy fillets in a sterilized preserving jar, making alternate layers of fish and salt until the jar is completely filled. Seal and store in a dark, dry place.
(See also recipe page 18.)

• Moroccan preserved lemons

Wash the lemons, slash the rind with a sharp knife and fill the slashes with coarse sea salt. Pack into a sterilized preserving jar, add 1 tablespoon coarse sea salt and seal. Place the jar in a dark, dry place.
(See also recipe page 74.)

• Sun-dried mushrooms

Using a needle and thread, pierce each mushroom near the base of the stalk and make a chain of them, knotting the thread after each mushroom so that they stay separate and do not fall on one another. Wrap the mushroom-chain in muslin and dry in the sun. When dry – wait at least 15 days – pack the mushrooms in a jar.

preserving in
olive oil

Fennel Oil

10 black peppercorns
5 juniper berries
12 fennel sprigs
750 ml (1¼ pints) olive oil

Drop the peppercorns and juniper berries into a
glass bottle. Carefully add the fennel sprigs, then
fill with olive oil. Seal the bottle with a cork and
leave to infuse for at least 2 weeks.

TIP: This oil is delicious with potato salad and
pickled herrings, or can also be used in a
marinade for salmon.

Garlic and Basil Oil

2 basil sprigs
3 garlic cloves
8 black peppercorns
4 coriander seeds
750 ml (1¼ pints) olive oil

Carefully remove the leaves from the basil sprigs
and leave them to dry in the sun or in your
kitchen for about 24 hours. Put them into a glass
bottle and add the garlic. Drop in the peppercorns
and coriander seeds, then fill the bottle with olive
oil. Seal with a cork and leave to infuse for at
least 2 weeks.

TIP: You can use this oil in a dressing for tomato
salad or crudités, or for flavouring pan-fried
steak or brushing on to meat before grilling.

Red Chilli Oil

about 10 small dried red chillies
4–5 thyme sprigs
3 oregano sprigs
10 black peppercorns
750 ml (1¼ pints) olive oil

Put the chillies into a glass bottle. Carefully add
the thyme and oregano sprigs. Drop in the black
peppercorns, then fill the bottle with olive oil.
Seal with a cork and leave to infuse for at least
2 weeks.

TIP: This spicy chilli-flavoured oil is a delicious
accompaniment to pizza, plainly grilled fish or
potato salad.

Oregano Oil

2–3 fresh oregano sprigs
or 2 tablespoons dried oregano
750 ml (1¼ pints) olive oil

Wash the oregano and gently pat it dry in a tea
towel or with kitchen paper. Drop the oregano
sprigs into a bottle, then fill with olive oil. Seal
with a cork, put the bottle in a dry, dark place
and leave for about 10 days before using.

TIP: This oil is excellent with pasta or pizza,
or to flavour grilled white meat.

Basil Oil

2–3 fresh basil sprigs
750 ml (1¼ pints) olive oil

Wash the basil, then pat it dry in a tea towel or
with kitchen paper. Drop the basil sprigs into a
bottle, and fill with olive oil. Seal with a cork, put
the bottle in a dry, dark place and leave for about
10 days before using.

TIP: This oil is a delicious seasoning for raw
tomatoes and tomato sauces.

Garlic Oil

4 garlic cloves, crushed
750 ml (1¼ pints) olive oil

Drop the garlic into the bottle and fill with olive
oil. Seal with a cork, put the bottle in a dry, dark
place and leave for about 10 days before using.

TIP: This oil is equally good for seasoning pasta,
slices of grilled meat or vegetable soup.

Goat's Cheese in Olive Oil

Preparation time: 5 minutes
No cooking required

10 small, fresh goat's cheeses
2 thyme sprigs
1 small bay leaf
12 black peppercorns
750 ml (1¼ pints) olive oil

Place the goat's cheeses in a preserving jar. Add the thyme, bay leaf and peppercorns. Cover with olive oil. Seal the jar with an airtight lid and leave it in a cool place, but not the refrigerator, as the cold will make the oil congeal. Leave for about 10 days before eating the cheeses.

TIP: Moisten some slices of crusty bread with the aromatic oil and serve them along with the goat's cheeses.

Goat's Cheese with Garlic and Savory

Preparation time: 5 minutes
No cooking required

3 savory sprigs
about 10 small goat's cheeses
2 garlic cloves
750 ml (1¼ pints) olive oil

Wash the savory, then pat it dry in a tea towel or with kitchen paper. Place some of the goat's cheeses at the bottom of a preserving jar and cover with savory sprigs. Add a garlic clove, then place another layer of cheeses on top and sprinkle with savory. Continue making layers in the same way until all the cheeses are in the jar. Pour in the olive oil, ensuring that it covers the cheeses. Seal the jar with an airtight lid and leave in a dark place for about 10 days before opening.

Miniature Goat's Cheese with Rosemary

Preparation time: 5 minutes
No cooking required

2–3 fresh rosemary sprigs
about 10 miniature goat's cheeses
750 ml (1¼ pints) olive oil

Wash the rosemary, then pat it dry in a tea towel or with kitchen paper. Place a few of the goat's cheeses at the bottom of a preserving jar, then cover with rosemary sprigs. Add another layer of cheeses and cover with rosemary. Continue in the same way until all the cheeses are in the jar. Pour in the olive oil, making sure that it covers the cheeses. Seal the jar with an airtight lid, then leave in a dark, dry place for about 10 days before opening.

Goat's Cheese in Olive Oil

Tuna-stuffed Red Peppers in Oil

Preparation time: 15 minutes
Cooking time: 2 minutes

375 g (12 oz) small red peppers
1 large can of tuna in oil
1 teaspoon black peppercorns
2 bay leaves
750 ml (1¼ pints)

Slit the peppers along 1 side and deseed. Bring a large saucepan of water to the boil, and drop in the peppers. Simmer for 2 minutes, then drain. Flake the tuna with a fork and use it to stuff the peppers. Place the peppers in a preserving jar with the peppercorns and bay leaves. Cover with olive oil and seal the jar with an airtight lid. Store in a dark place.

Dried Tomatoes in Oil

Preparation time: 15 minutes
Cooking time: 1½ hours

500 g (1 lb) small, very ripe tomatoes, halved and deseeded
1 bay leaf
1 tablespoon white wine vinegar
750 ml (1¼ pints) olive oil

Place the tomatoes in a preheated oven, 120°C (250°F), Gas Mark ½, for about 1½ hours, then remove from the oven and leave to cool.
Put the tomatoes in a preserving jar with the bay leaf. Pour in the vinegar and cover with olive oil. Seal the jar with an airtight lid.
Leave in a dark place, checking from time to time to ensure that the tomatoes are still covered in oil. Once the jar is opened, store in a cool place.

TIP: This recipe is even better if you can sun-dry your tomatoes, as people do in many Mediterranean countries such as Italy, Spain and Tunisia. To do this, place the quartered tomatoes on a tray and expose them directly to the sun, at the same time taking care to ensure that they are protected from dust. Leave them for several days, turning them over regularly and bringing them indoors every night to avoid damp.

Tuna-stuffed Red Peppers in Oil

Anchovy Double

In Salt

Preparation time: 45 minutes + 8 days standing
No cooking required

1 kg (2 lb) anchovies
1 kg (2 lb) cooking salt
peppercorns
bay leaves
cloves

Rinse the anchovies in cold water, then drain well. Using a small, sharp knife, cut off the heads and fillet the fish.

Place the anchovies in a large, shallow dish and cover with half the cooking salt. Stir well to make sure that they are thoroughly coated in salt. Leave to stand overnight.

Sterilize a preserving jar by placing it in a large pan of boiling water for 5 minutes, then place it upside down on a clean tea towel to drain. Pour a layer of cooking salt into the bottom of the dry jar and arrange some anchovies, belly side down, on top. Add 6 peppercorns, ½ bay leaf and 2 cloves. Spoon in another layer of salt, then add another layer of anchovies with peppercorns, ½ bay leaf and cloves on top. Continue making layers in this way until the jar is full.

Close the lid of the jar and place a weight on top. Leave to stand for 1 week in a cool, dark place. Open the jar and remove the oil that has formed on the surface. Pour in a little cooking salt in its place. Seal the jar with an airtight lid and leave it in a cool, dark place.

Store for about 3 weeks before opening and eating the salted anchovies.

TIP: You can use the anchovies as and when you need them, taking care to rinse them under cold running water, remove their backbones and leave them to soak for at least 1 hour in a bowl of cold water.

In Oil

After you have left the anchovies to stand in salt for 1 week, remove the anchovy fillets, 1 at a time, and wipe each of them with kitchen paper. Sterilize a preserving jar for 5 minutes in a large saucepan of boiling water, then place it upside down on a clean tea towel to drain.

Put the anchovy fillets in the dry jar, and cover them with olive oil. Close and sterilize the jar for 1½ hours, then leave it to cool. Sterilize for a further 30 minutes the following day.

TIP: You can put these anchovies in a salade niçoise or pan-bagnat – both specialities from the south of France. You can also use them to make anchovy butter, or purée them and serve them in an anchoïade with fresh vegetables.

Anchovies in Oil

Marinated Feta

Cut some feta cheese into small cubes. Sterilize a preserving jar, then leave it upside down on a clean tea towel to drain. Put the feta in the dry jar, cover with an aromatic olive oil and seal. You can use this feta to liven up your salads.

Farfalle Salad

To vary pasta salads, add some drained diced Dried Tomatoes in Oil (see page 16), diced celery and some capers, then season with a good olive oil vinaigrette.

Oil for Pizza

To spice up your pizza parties, offer your guests some Red Chilli Oil (see page 12). Take care though – as time goes by it gets hotter and hotter, so just a few drops will be enough.

Mini-pizzas

Use a biscuit cutter to stamp out 12 rounds of pizza dough. Cover the rounds with a garlic and onion tomato sauce which you have prepared earlier. Lay a slice of mozzarella on each round, and sprinkle with chopped oregano. Add a strip of green, red or yellow pepper and an olive. Finally, brush the mini-pizzas with olive oil. Cook for about 12 minutes in a preheated oven, 200°C (400°F), Gas Mark 6.

Barbecuing

In the barbecue season, dip a pastry brush in some Garlic and Basil Oil (see page 12), and lightly brush some pork chops on both sides. Barbecue them for about 12 minutes, turning them over halfway through the cooking time. Serve immediately with a green salad.

Tomatoes with Mozzarella

Slice some tomatoes, then cover with slices of mozzarella and sprinkle with Basil Oil (see page 12). Season with salt and pepper and top with more tomato slices. Serve immediately. You can also add some black olives and a few fresh basil leaves.

Potato Salad

Peel some boiled potatoes while they are still warm. Cut them into round slices. Add 6 small spring onions cut into quarters, then toss lightly with a vinaigrette made with Oregano Oil (see page 12). You can also give extra flavour to your salad by adding a small amount of chopped garlic.

Carpaccio of Beef

Put a piece of fillet steak in the freezer for
10–15 minutes to firm it, then cut it into wafer-
thin slices. Lightly brush a large plate with Basil
Oil (see page 12). Arrange the beef slices on the
plate, brush with more oil, then season to taste
with salt and pepper.

TIP: You can also sprinkle on a little coarsely
grated Parmesan cheese.

Spicy Prawns

Place some cooked peeled prawns in a deep
dish. In a bowl, mix together some olive oil and
Red Chilli Oil (see page 12) to taste. Pour the
mixture over the prawns and leave to marinate
for at least 2 hours.

TIP: You can serve the prawns just as they are
with pre-dinner drinks, or use them to add
interest to a green salad or fried rice.

Marinated Chicken Drumsticks

Place some chicken drumsticks in a deep dish.
In a jug, mix together some Garlic Oil
(see page 12) and Red Chilli Oil (see page 12),
using about twice as much of the former as
the latter. Pour the mixture over the drumsticks
to cover. Add some chopped coriander leaves.
Leave to marinate for at least 2 hours, then cook
the drumsticks in the oven or on the barbecue.

Diced Cod with Fennel Oil

Cut a fillet of cod into large cubes, place in a
deep dish and cover with Fennel Oil (see page
12). Leave to marinate for at least 2 hours.
Cook a chopped onion in oil until lightly
browned, add the cubes of marinated fish
and cook over a medium heat until tender.
Season to taste with salt and pepper.

TIP: Just before serving, sprinkle with lemon
juice and a little chopped fresh fennel.

Carpaccio of Beef

Fennel Salmon with Mustard Sauce

Preparation time: 10 minutes
+ 2 hours marinating
No cooking required
4 servings

400 g (13 oz) sliced smoked salmon
Fennel Oil (see page 12)
1 tablespoon crushed white peppercorns
For the sauce
1 teaspoon caster sugar
1 teaspoon chopped fennel
1 tablespoon mild mustard
1 teaspoon white wine vinegar
4 tablespoons sunflower oil

Arrange the salmon slices in a large, deep dish.
Pour over fennel oil to cover and sprinkle with the
crushed white peppercorns. Cover with clingfilm
and place in the refrigerator for at least 2 hours.
Just before serving, prepare the sauce. Mix
together the caster sugar, chopped fennel and
mustard in a bowl, add the vinegar, then
gradually pour in the sunflower oil, stirring
constantly. Serve the fish with the sauce.

Fennel Salmon with Mustard Sauce

Grilled Garlic Chicken Breasts

Preparation time: 10 minutes
Cooking time: 6 minutes
4 servings

2 skinless boneless chicken breasts, cut into
thin strips
1 tablespoon Garlic Oil (see page 12)
a few basil leaves
200 g (7 oz) lettuce leaves
3 small white onions, thinly sliced
3 tablespoons olive oil
1½ teaspoons Honey Vinegar (see page 36)
salt and pepper

Brush the chicken strips with a little garlic oil and
season with salt and pepper.
Cook under a preheated grill, turning frequently,
for about 6 minutes, until golden on all sides.
Meanwhile, place the basil leaves and lettuce
in a large salad bowl and add the onions.
Whisk together the olive oil and vinegar in a jug.
Pour the dressing over the salad, then season
lightly with salt and pepper. Toss well to mix.
Arrange the grilled chicken strips on the salad
and serve immediately.

Grilled Garlic Chicken Breasts

Grilled Goat's Cheese on Toast

Preparation time: 5 minutes
Cooking time: 4–5 minutes
4 servings

4 slices of crusty bread
or ½ baguette
2 cabécou or other individual goat's
cheeses marinated in oil, drained and
halved horizontally
pepper

Lightly toast the bread on 1 side under a
preheated grill. Remove from the heat and
arrange the cheese on top. Return to the grill
and cook until the cheese has melted.
Season lightly with pepper and serve with a
mixed green or rocket salad.

Grilled Goat's Cheese on Toast

Dried Tomato and Olive Oil Paste

Preparation time: 15 minutes
No cooking required

200 g (7 oz) dried tomatoes
200 ml (7 fl oz) water
1 bay leaf
olive oil

Place the dried tomatoes in a small pan, add the measured water and heat gently for about 10 minutes. Transfer to a blender or food processor and process to a thick paste. If necessary add a little extra water.
Pour the tomato paste into a preserving jar and add the bay leaf. Cover with a little olive oil. Seal the jar with an airtight lid and store in a dark cupboard. Once the jar has been opened, keep the tomato and olive oil paste in a cool place.

Pizzas with Dried Tomato Paste and Anchovies

Preparation time: 20 minutes
+ 1 hour rising time for the dough
Cooking time: 12 minutes
4 servings

Garlic Oil (see page 12)
Dried Tomato and Olive Oil Paste (see left)
20 canned anchovy fillets, drained
1 teaspoon oregano
olive oil, for brushing
For the dough
1 sachet baker's yeast
150 ml (¼ pint) lukewarm water
250 g (8 oz) plain flour
1 tablespoon olive oil
salt

First, make the dough. Mix the yeast with 2 tablespoons of the water in a small bowl. Put the flour and a pinch of salt into a food processor, add the yeast mixture and process to mix. With the motor running, gradually add the remaining water and the olive oil. As soon as the mixture comes together, turn out the dough and knead until smooth and elastic. Place the dough on a baking sheet, cover with a tea towel and leave to rise in a warm, draught-free place for about 1 hour, or until doubled in volume.
Brush a baking sheet with oil, then sprinkle lightly with flour.
Divide the dough into 4 equal balls and place on the baking sheet. Gently flatten with your hand to form 4 rounds of equal size. Set the rounds aside for about 10 minutes.
Brush the dough rounds with garlic oil, then spread the tomato paste over them.
Divide the anchovy fillets among the pizzas, sprinkle with oregano and brush with olive oil. Bake in a preheated oven, 200°C (400°F), Gas Mark 6, for about 12 minutes. Serve immediately.

Pizzas with Dried Tomato Paste and Anchovies

preserving
in vinegar

Myrtle and Blackberry Vinegar

1 handful of blackberries, preferably wild
1 small myrtle sprig
1 litre (1¾ pints) wine vinegar

Gently insert the blackberries and sprig of myrtle into a bottle, pour in wine vinegar and seal the bottle well.
Store in a dark, dry place.
Leave for about 3 weeks before using.

TIP: Excellent for deglazing the roasting tin after cooking game. It is well worth trying to obtain myrtle for this recipe, as it is a lovely, fragrant, spicy herb, but it is not widely available. You could substitute rosemary or lavender instead.

Rosemary Vinegar

1 large rosemary sprig
1 litre (1¾ pints) wine vinegar

Put the rosemary sprig into the bottle,
pour in the vinegar and seal the bottle well.
Store in a dark, dry place.
Leave for at least 3 weeks before using.

TIP: Excellent with grilled or pan-fried meat or with steamed fish.

Tarragon Vinegar

5 tarragon sprigs
1 litre (1¾ pints) wine vinegar

Dry the sprigs of tarragon in a dark, dry place for 1 week.
Insert the dried tarragon into a bottle, pour in the vinegar and seal the bottle well.
Store in a dark, dry place.
Leave for at least 3 weeks before using.

TIP: This vinegar goes well in robust salads, with chicken dishes or as a seasoning for fried eggs.

Basil Vinegar

1 large basil sprig
1 litre (1¾ pints) wine vinegar

Place the basil in a bottle, pour in the vinegar and seal well.
Store in a dark, dry place.
Leave for at least 3 weeks before using.

TIP: This vinegar makes an excellent salad dressing with olive oil.

Rosemary Vinegar; Myrtle and Blackberry Vinegar

Honey Vinegar

**4 tablespoons clear honey
1 litre (1¾ pints) cider vinegar**

Pour the honey and vinegar into a bottle and seal well.
Store the bottle in a dark, dry place.
Leave for about 3 weeks before using.

TIP: This vinegar is delicious in salad dressings, good for spicing up apple sauce, and can also be used to deglaze roasting tins for making gravy – especially with duck.

Fruit Vinegar

**1 handful of slightly under-ripe berries, such as strawberries or raspberries
5 small bay leaves
1 litre (1¾ pints) wine vinegar**

Put the berries and bay leaves in a bottle, pour in the vinegar and seal the bottle well.
Store in a dark, dry place.
Leave about 3 weeks before using.

TIP: Excellent in a vinaigrette or to season a fresh green salad. The berries will go on ripening in the bottle and will end up a very attractive red.

Honey Vinegar

Pickled Onions

Pickled Cherries

Pickled Onions

Preparation time: 20 minutes + cooling
Cooking time: 5 minutes

500 g (1 lb) pickling onions
1 clove
1 bay leaf
5 black peppercorns
500 ml (17 fl oz) white wine vinegar

Bring a saucepan of water to the boil. Add the onions and boil for 2 minutes. Drain well and place them in a preserving jar together with the clove, bay leaf and peppercorns.
Pour the vinegar into a heavy-based saucepan. Bring to the boil and boil for 3 minutes, then remove from the heat and leave to cool.
Pour the vinegar into the jar to cover the onions seal the jar with an airtight lid.
Store in a dark, dry place for about 2 months before consuming.

Pickled Cherries

Preparation time: 10 minutes + cooling
Cooking time: 5 minutes

500 g (1 lb) cherries
600 ml (1 pint) cider vinegar
100 g (3½ oz) granulated sugar
2 cloves
¼ cinnamon stick
¼ teaspoon ground nutmeg

Place the cherries in a preserving jar.
Pour the vinegar into a heavy-based saucepan and add the sugar, cloves, the cinnamon and nutmeg. Bring to the boil and boil for 3 minutes, then remove from the heat and leave to cool.
Pour the vinegar mixture into the jar to cover the cherries seal the jar with an airtight lid.
Store in a dark, dry, place for about 2 months before consuming the cherries.

Pickled Gherkins with Tarragon

Preparation time: 25 minutes
+ overnight standing
No cooking required

1 kg (2 lb) small gherkins, trimmed
300 g (10 oz) coarse sea salt
4 shallots
10 fresh or dried tarragon sprigs
15 black peppercorns
15 coriander seeds
1 litre (1¾ pints) distilled malt vinegar

Rub the gherkins vigorously in a towel to remove any down.
Place them in a large bowl and cover with the salt, mixing well to ensure that they are thoroughly coated. Leave overnight for the juices to drain.
Next day, drain the gherkins and pat dry with a tea towel or kitchen paper.
Put the gherkins into preserving jars. Divide the shallots, tarragon, peppercorns and coriander seeds among the jars. Pour in the vinegar and seal the jars with airtight lids.
Store in a dark, dry place for 6–8 weeks before eating gherkins.

TIP: These gherkins are delicious with pâté or cold meat. They can also be added, cut into rounds, into a potato salad garnished with a shallot vinaigrette. Some people like to heat the vinegar before pouring it over the gherkins, but the use of cold vinegar appears to produce a tastier result: the gherkins are then incomparably crunchy.

Pickled Gherkins with Tarragon

Spiced Pickled Red Cabbage

**Preparation time: 20 minutes
+ overnight standing
Cooking time: 3 minutes**

1 kg (2 lb) red cabbage, cored and shredded
1 litre (1¾ pints) red wine vinegar
10 black peppercorns
4 bay leaves
6 cloves
salt

Place the cabbage in a large terrine and cover
with salt. Mix well and leave overnight.
Next day, drain the cabbage and pat dry with
kitchen paper to remove the salt. Pour the vinegar
and spices into a heavy-based saucepan. Bring to
the boil and boil for 3 minutes; then remove
the saucepan from the heat. Pack the cabbage
strips into preserving jars and pour in the spiced
vinegar to cover. Seal the jars with airtight lids.
Store in a dark, dry place for at least 2 weeks
before eating.
This makes a splendid garnish with a pie.

Pickled Beetroot

**Preparation time: 20 minutes + cooling
Cooking time: about 2½ hours**

500 g (1 lb) beetroot
500 ml (17 fl oz) wine vinegar
1 clove
1 bay leaf
5 black peppercorns
salt

Sterilize a preserving jar in a large saucepan of
boiling water for 5 minutes, then put it upside
down to drain on a clean tea towel.
Put the beetroot in a saucepan and add water to
cover. Add a pinch of salt and bring to the boil.
Lower the heat and simmer for 2 hours, until
tender. Check by inserting the point of a sharp
knife in the thickest part; it should slide in easily.
Remove the beetroot from the saucepan and
leave to cool. Peel and slice.
Place the slices in the dry jar with the clove, bay
leaf and peppercorns. Pour the wine vinegar into
a heavy-based saucepan. Bring to the boil and
boil for 3 minutes, then remove from the heat.
Pour the vinegar into the jar to cover the beetroot
and seal the jar with an airtight lid.
Store in a dark, dry place for 2 weeks before
consuming.

Pickled Beetroot

Pickled Pearl Onions

**Preparation time: 20 minutes
+ 2 hours standing
Cooking time: 15 minutes**

500 g (1 lb) pearl onions
50 g (2 oz) coarse sea salt
600 ml (1 pint) cider vinegar
1 teaspoon mustard seeds
1 teaspoon coriander seeds
3 cloves
½ cinnamon stick
5 black peppercorns

Bring a large saucepan of water to the boil, add the onions and cook for 2 minutes. Drain well, place in a dish and cover them with the sea salt. Set aside for about 2 hours.

Pour the cider vinegar into a saucepan and add the mustard seeds, coriander seeds, cloves, cinnamon and the peppercorns. Bring to the boil and boil for about 3 minutes. Remove the pan from the heat and leave to cool.

Rinse the onions to remove the salt, then place them in a heavy-based pan. Pour in the spiced vinegar and bring to the boil. Simmer for about 6 minutes, then remove the pan from the heat. Pack the onions in a preserving jar, pour in spiced vinegar to cover and seal with an airtight lid. Store in a dark, dry place for at least 2 weeks before consuming.

Miniature Pickled Vegetables

**Preparation time: 20 minutes
Cooking time: 10 minutes**

200 g (7 oz) small French beans, cut into 2.5 cm (1 inch) lengths
200 g (7 oz) pearl onions
200 g (7 oz) cauliflower florets
600 ml (1 pint) malt vinegar
1 teaspoon mustard powder
1 teaspoon grated fresh root ginger

Sterilize a jar in a saucepan of boiling water for 5 minutes, then put it upside down to drain on a clean tea towel.

Bring a large pan of salted water to the boil, add the French beans, onions and cauliflower and cook for 2 minutes. Drain well and place the vegetables in a preserving jar.

Pour the malt vinegar into a saucepan and add the mustard powder and ginger. Bring to the boil, then lower the heat and simmer for about 3 minutes. Remove the pan from the heat and strain the vinegar into a jug. Pour the vinegar into the jar to cover the miniature vegetables, then seal the jar with an airtight lid.

Store in a dark dry place for at least 2 weeks before using.

TIP: You can pickle other vegetables in the same way. Try baby corn cobs, slices of carrot, small gherkins, and chunks of red pepper.

Miniature Pickled Vegetables

Pickled Mushrooms

Preparation time: 20 minutes + cooling
Cooking time: 20 minutes

500 g (1 lb) mushrooms
250 ml (8 fl oz) white wine vinegar
250 ml (8 fl oz) white wine
250 ml (8 fl oz) water
1 thyme sprig
½ teaspoon mustard seeds
3 black peppercorns
2 tablespoons caster sugar
1¼ teaspoons salt

Cut any large mushrooms into quarters.
Pour the vinegar, wine and water into a heavy-based saucepan. Add the thyme, mustard seeds, peppercorns, sugar and salt.
Bring to the boil and add the mushrooms. Lower the heat and simmer for about 8 minutes.
Remove the mushrooms with a slotted spoon, and continue to simmer the vinegar mixture for a further 5 minutes, until reduced. Remove from the heat and leave to cool.
Sterilize a preserving jar in a large saucepan of boiling water for 5 minutes, then put it upside down to drain on a clean tea towel. Fill the jar with the mushrooms and pour in the cooled vinegar mixture. Seal the jar with an airtight lid. Store in a dark, dry place.

TIP: These mushrooms are an excellent garnish for dry-cured ham.

Chanterelle Mushrooms in Vinegar

Preparation time: 15 minutes
Cooking time: 1 hour

500 g (1 lb) small chanterelle mushrooms
1 shallot
1 thyme sprig
5 peppercorns
1¼ teaspoons salt
250 ml (8 fl oz) white wine vinegar
250 ml (8 fl oz) water

Cut any large mushrooms in half, then place all the mushrooms in a preserving jar. Add the shallot, thyme, peppercorns and salt.
Pour the vinegar and water into a heavy-based saucepan. Bring to the boil, then lower the heat and simmer for 2–3 minutes. Pour the mixture into the jar and seal with an airtight lid.
Place the jar in a large saucepan, add enough water to cover and bring to the boil. Boil for 1 hour. Remove the jar from the pan and leave to cool completely.
Store the jar in a dark, dry place.

TIP: These mushrooms make an excellent garnish for pork dishes.

Pickled Mushrooms

Home-pickled Gherkins

For lunch on the run, you can't beat
the traditional crusty sandwich, with
fresh baguette, good-quality salami
or salt beef, unsalted butter and a
handful of Pickled Gherkins with
Tarragon (see page 40). They are also
incomparable on a platter of cold
meats. Try them, too, with venison
or other strongly flavoured pâté.

Fruit Vinegar

For a pleasant change, substitute
the delicate taste of Fruit Vinegar (see
page 36) for wine vinegar when
dressing a green salad. You will better
appreciate its fragrance if you prepare
the vinaigrette with a neutral-tasting
oil, such as sunflower oil, for instance.

Pickled Cherries

Pickled Cherries (see page 40) have a unique sharp crunchiness. They lend piquancy to cold meats and are a marvellous accompaniment to a good terrine or coarse pâté.

Pickled Mushrooms

You could surprise guests by serving Pickled Mushrooms (see page 46) on cocktail sticks with pre-dinner drinks. You could then go on to serve them as a first-course garnish to spice up game pâté, for example.

Pickled Onions

You have some left-over roast beef? Now's the time to get out your Pickled Pearl Onions (see page 44).

Fried Egg with Fruit Vinegar

Preparation time: 5 minutes
Cooking time: 2–3 minutes
1 Serving

knob of butter
½ teaspoon sunflower oil
1 or 2 eggs
Fruit Vinegar (see page 36)
salt and pepper

Melt the butter with the oil in a small, nonstick frying pan.
Crack the egg or eggs into it and cook over a low heat for a few minutes, until the white is cooked and set but the yolk is still runny. Season lightly with salt and pepper and transfer to a plate. Add a dash of fruit vinegar and serve.

TIP: This is even more delicious served with crusty country bread or fresh baguette.

Fried Egg with Fruit Vinegar

Tarragon Vinaigrette with Shallots

1 teaspoon Dijon mustard
1 tablespoon Tarragon Vinegar (see page 34)
3 tablespoons sunflower oil
1 shallot, chopped
salt and pepper

Place the mustard and vinegar in a bowl, season with salt and stir briskly with a fork or small whisk. Gradually add the oil, whisking constantly until thoroughly combined. Add the chopped shallot and season with pepper. Use immediately to dress a potato salad, for example.

Garlic and Rosemary Vinaigrette

1 tablespoon Rosemary Vinegar (see page 34)
3 tablespoons Garlic Oil (see page 12)
salt and pepper

Pour the vinegar into a bowl, season with salt and whisk well. Gradually add the oil, whisking constantly until thoroughly combined. Season with pepper and use immediately to dress a green salad, for example.

Curry-flavoured Vinaigrette

2 teaspoons curry powder
1 tablespoon white wine vinegar
3 tablespoons Garlic Oil (see page 12)
salt and pepper

Put the curry powder and vinegar in a bowl, season with salt and stir well with a fork or small whisk. Gradually add the oil, stirring constantly until thoroughly combined. Season with pepper, and use immediately to dress a beetroot or potato salad or steamed leeks.

Curry-flavoured Vinaigrette

Duck Fillets with Honey Vinegar

Preparation time: 5 minutes
Cooking time: 15 minutes
4 Servings

2 duck breast fillets
1 tablespoon Honey Vinegar (see page 36)
salt and pepper

Lightly score the skin of the duck breasts with a small, sharp knife.

Season the flesh side of the duck with salt and pepper. Heat a heavy-based frying pan. Add the duck breasts, skin side down and cook for about 10 minutes.

Drain off the fat from the pan and turn the duck breasts over. Cook for a further 3–4 minutes, then remove the duck breasts from the pan and keep warm.

Drain off the fat from the pan and pour in the honey vinegar. Heat gently, scraping the base of the pan with a wooden spoon to release the meat juices into the vinegar.

Serve the duck immediately with the honey vinegar-flavoured juices poured over.

TIP: Depending on season and price, you can vary the choice of vegetables served with this dish.

Pickled Vegetable Mini-kebabs

Preparation time: 20 minutes
+ overnight standing
Cooking time: 10 minutes

250 g (8 oz) gherkins
250 g (8 oz) red peppers, halved
and deseeded
250 g (8 oz) carrots, cut into quarters
250 g (8 oz) pearl onions
1 litre (1¾ pints) distilled malt vinegar
10 black peppercorns
salt

Put the gherkins in a large dish and cover with a fine layer of salt. Put the pepper halves in another dish and cover with a fine layer of salt.

The following day, wipe the peppers with kitchen paper to remove the excess salt, then cut them into small squares. Wipe the gherkins.

Bring a large saucepan of water to the boil, add the carrots and cook for 3–4 minutes. Drain well. Cook the pearl onions in a pan of boiling water for 1 minute, then drain well.

Thread the vegetables on to small wooden skewers, alternating carrots, onions, pepper squares and gherkins.

Place the mini-kebabs together vertically in large preserving jars. Pour in the vinegar and add the peppercorns. Seal the jars with airtight lids.

Store in a dark place for about 3 weeks before serving the mini-kebabs, which will be delicious either as canapés with pre-dinner drinks or as an accompaniment to cold meat or pâté.

TIP: If you have any pickled mushrooms, such as small chanterelles, add these to your kebabs. You can add pitted olives too.

Pickled Vegetable Mini-kebabs

sweet-and-sour preserves

Onion Marmalade

Preparation time: 10 minutes
Cooking time: 45 minutes

500 g (1 lb) onions, thinly sliced
125 ml (4 fl oz) wine vinegar
250 ml (8 fl oz) red wine
100 g (3½ oz) caster sugar
250 ml (8 fl oz) grenadine
salt and pepper

Place the onions in a large, nonstick frying-pan, cover and cook over a very low heat for about 10 minutes.
Pour in the vinegar and red wine, increase the heat to high and cook, uncovered, for 5 minutes, until reduced.
Lower the heat and add the sugar and grenadine. Season with salt and pepper.
Stir well and simmer very gently for 30 minutes. The mixture will gradually thicken. Remove from the heat and leave to cool slightly.
Pour into jars and seal while still warm.

TIP: Serve the onion marmalade with cold meat or duck pâté.

Sweet-and-Sour Gherkins

Preparation time: 15 minutes
Cooking time: 40 minutes

½ carrot, sliced
1 white onion, thinly sliced
a few fennel sprigs
5 coriander seeds
5 black peppercorns
500 g (1 lb) large gherkins
100 ml (3½ fl oz) white wine vinegar
400 ml (14 fl oz) water
20 g (¾ oz) caster sugar
1½ teaspoons fine salt

Sterilize a preserving jar in a large pan of boiling water for 5 minutes. Leave upside down to drain on a tea towel. Put the carrot and onion slices into the dry jar with the fennel, coriander seeds, peppercorns and gherkins.
Pour the vinegar and water into a heavy-based saucepan and add the sugar and salt. Bring to the boil, then immediately remove the pan from the heat. Leave the brine to cool slightly, then pour into the jar to cover the gherkins. Seal the jar, place in a large saucepan of water and bring to the boil. Boil for about 30 minutes.
Leave the jar to cool in the saucepan, then store it in a cool, dark place.

TIP: Wait for about 1 month before opening.

Onion Marmalade

Mostarda

**Preparation time: 15 minutes
+ overnight standing
Cooking time: 20 minutes**

250 g (8 oz) caster sugar
1 litre (1¾ pints) water
4 slightly firm pears, peeled, cored and cut
into chunks
4 apples, peeled, cored and cut into chunks
4 slightly firm plums
12 grapes
750 ml (1¼ pints) white wine
500 g (1 lb) honey
25 g (1 oz) mustard powder

Put the caster sugar into a heavy-based saucepan,
pour in the water and heat gently, stirring until
the sugar has dissolved.
Add the pears and apples and simmer for about
10 minutes. Add the plums and grapes and
simmer for a further 5 minutes. Remove from the
heat, and leave the mixture to stand overnight.
The following day, bring the contents of the pan
back to simmering point, then strain the fruits
and pack them into preserving jars.
Pour the wine and honey into another heavy-
based saucepan, add the mustard powder and
heat to simmering point. Pour mixture into the
jars to cover the fruit and seal the jars with
airtight lids.

TIP: This mostarda will keep for several weeks,
and may be served with boiled or roast meat.

Mango Chutney

**Preparation time: 15 minutes
+ about 3 hours standing
Cooking time: 2½ hours
Makes 2 jars (250 g/8 oz each)**

3 mangoes, peeled, pitted and diced
(see page 6)
200 g (7 oz) soft brown sugar
1 pinch ground turmeric
1 teaspoon ground cinnamon
1 teaspoon grated fresh root ginger
½ teaspoon salt
2 garlic cloves, chopped
1 large onion, thinly sliced
400 ml (14 fl oz) malt or white wine vinegar

Put the mangoes, sugar, turmeric, cinnamon and ginger into a dish. Mix well and leave to stand for about 2 hours.
Transfer the mixture to a heavy-based saucepan, add the salt, garlic, onion and vinegar and bring to simmering point, stirring constantly. Simmer, stirring occasionally, for about 2½ hours, until the chutney has thickened.
Sterilize 2 preserving jars in a large saucepan of boiling water for 5 minutes, then remove and place upside down on a clean tea towel to drain. Leave the chutney to stand for about 20 minutes, then ladle it into the jars, and seal with airtight lids. Turn the jars upside down. When cool, store in a cool dark place.

TIP: You can use this chutney immediately, but it will be even better if you leave it for a fortnight. Once a jar has been opened it will keep very well for 2 weeks in the refrigerator.

Apple and Raisin Chutney

**Preparation time: 10 minutes
+ 1½ hours standing
Cooking time: 2½ hours
Makes 3 jars (250 g/8 oz each)**

500 g (1 lb) apples, peeled, quartered and cored
1 large onion, thinly sliced
200 g (7 oz) raisins
200 g (7 oz) soft brown sugar
1 teaspoon grated fresh root ginger
½ teaspoon salt
300 ml (½ pint) cider vinegar

Thinly slice the apple quarters crossways and place in a dish. Add the onion, raisins, sugar, ginger, salt and vinegar and leave to stand for about 1 hour. Pour the contents of the dish into a heavy-based saucepan and heat to simmering point, stirring constantly. Simmer, stirring occasionally, for about 2½ hours, until thickened. Sterilize 3 preserving jars in a large saucepan of boiling water for 5 minutes, then remove and place upside down to drain on a clean tea towel. Leave the chutney to stand for about 20 minutes, then ladle it into the jars and seal with airtight lids. Turn the jars upside down. When cool, store in a cool, dark place.

TIP: You can use the chutney immediately, but it will be even better if you leave it for a fortnight. Once a jar has been opened, keep it in the refrigerator.

Mango Chutney

Orange and Date Chutney

Preparation time: 10 minutes
+ 20 minutes standing
Cooking time: 2½ hours
Makes 3 jars (250 g/8 oz each)

375 g (12 oz) apples, peeled, quartered
and cored
200 g (7 oz) dates, pitted and chopped
150 g (5 oz) oranges, peeled and chopped
200 g (7 oz) soft brown sugar
2 teaspoons grated fresh root ginger
½ teaspoon salt
300 ml (½ pint) malt or white wine vinegar

Slice the apples into a heavy-based saucepan and
add the dates, oranges, sugar, ginger, salt and
vinegar. Bring to simmering point, stirring
constantly. Simmer, stirring occasionally, for about
2½ hours, until thickened.
Sterilize 3 preserving jars in a large saucepan of
boiling water for 5 minutes, then place upside
down on a clean tea towel to drain.
Leave the chutney to stand for about 20 minutes,
then ladle it into the jars and seal with airtight
lids. Turn the jars upside down. When cool, store
in a cool, dark place.

TIP: You can use this chutney immediately, but it
will be even better if you leave it for a fortnight.
Once a jar has been opened it must be kept in
the refrigerator.

Orange and Date Chutney

Boiled Beef with Mostarda

If you are wondering how to use a nice piece of boiled beef or some leftover braised steak, cut it into large cubes and serve it as a starter with some mustard-flavoured fruits. The Mostarda (see page 60) will lift the flavour of the cold meat deliciously.

Onion Marmalade

Onion Marmalade (see page 58) is the perfect accompaniment to ham, salami and other cold meats. It balances the flavours and is particularly good with game pâtés. You can also serve it with duck and farmhouse cheese.

Apple and Raisin Rice

Put 200 g (7 oz) basmati rice into a saucepan with 350 ml (12 fl oz) boiling water and season with salt and pepper. Cover and simmer for about 15 minutes, until tender. Strain the rice, if necessary, and serve warm with Apple and Raisin Chutney (see page 62). You could also add some slices of fresh mango.

Orange and Date Chutney

Put a boned and rolled loin of pork into a pan, cover with a mixture of milk and water, season and add 4 garlic cloves and 1 thyme sprig. Simmer, allowing 1¼ hours per 1 kg (2lb) meat. Drain and leave to cool. Slice and serve cold with Orange and Date Chutney (see page 64).

Sweet-and-Sour Mushrooms with Parma Ham

Sweet-and-sour mushrooms will make Parma ham, terrines and pâtés that little bit more special. The wild mushrooms will lose something of their rustic simplicity, but will make up for it by bringing out the delicious flavours of your cold meats.

Turkey Breast with Mango Chutney

Cut the turkey breast into short strips, then grill until tender and serve with Mango Chutney (see page 62) as a dipping sauce. You can also use these ingredients to make an absolutely delicious sandwich.

Duck and Hazelnut Pâté

Duck and Hazelnut Pâté

**Preparation time: 30 minutes
+ overnight marinating + 1–2 hours cooling
Cooking time: 2½ hours
Prepare the day before serving**

100 g (3½ oz) chicken livers
250 ml (8 fl oz) brandy
875 g (1¾ lb) duck breast fillets, cut into
large cubes
100 g (3½ oz) sausagemeat
220 g (7½ oz) belly pork
1 garlic clove, finely chopped
3 shallots, finely chopped
2 tablespoons chopped parsley
pinch of ground allspice
200 g (7 oz) shelled and skinned
hazelnuts, coarsely crushed
3 eggs, lightly beaten
200 g (7½ oz) fatty bacon or bacon fat
2 bay leaves
1 thyme sprig
salt and ground white pepper

Place the chicken livers in a deep dish, pour in the
brandy, cover and leave to marinate overnight in
a cool place.

The next day, drain the chicken livers. Pass the
duck, sausagemeat, belly pork and chicken livers
through a mincer or chop finely in a food
processor. Transfer to a bowl, if necessary.

Add the garlic, shallots and chopped parsley.
Season with salt, pepper and allspice, then add
the nuts and eggs. Mix thoroughly.

Place a layer of bacon or bacon fat in the base of
a 25-cm (10-inch) long terrine, and cover with the
duck mixture, packing it down firmly. Cover with
another layer of bacon or bacon fat. Decorate
with the bay leaves and the thyme sprig.

Put the terrine in a roasting tin and add boiling
water to come halfway up the sides.

Bake in a preheated oven, 160°C (325°F), Gas
Mark 3, for about 2½ hours, topping up with
more boiling water if necessary. Remove the
terrine from the roasting tin and leave to stand
for 1–2 hours at room temperature.

Cover the pâté with a small board, place a weight
on top and leave for about 12 hours. Store the
pâté in a cool place.

TIP: Serve with Onion Marmalade (see page 58).

preserving
with salt

Moroccan Preserved Lemons

Green Olives

Preparation time: 45 minutes + cooling
Cooking time: 5 minutes

500 g (1 lb) green olives
salt

Sterilize the jars in a large saucepan of boiling
water for 5 minutes, then leave to drain upside
down on a clean tea towel.
Put the olives in jars and pour in cold water to
cover. Leaving the olives in the jars, pour the
water into a measuring jug. Stir salt into the
water, in the proportion of 100 g (3½ oz) salt per
1 litre (1¾ pints) of water.
Pour the salted water into a saucepan and bring
to the boil. Boil for about 5 minutes, then remove
from the heat and leave to cool.
Pour the salt water on to the olives making sure
that they are completely covered in the liquid.
Leave to macerate for about 4 weeks before
consuming.

TIP: You can add aromatic interest to the olives
by adding a peeled garlic clove or a few strands
of fennel.
You can preserve black olives in the same way.

Moroccan Preserved Lemons

Preparation time: 10 minutes
No cooking required

10 unwaxed or thoroughly scrubbed lemons
fine salt
1 tablespoon coarse sea salt

Place in a deep dish and pour in cold water to
cover. Leave for about 6 days, changing the water
daily. Make incisions into the rind, as if cutting
them into quarters, but do not cut into the flesh.
Place a good pinch of fine salt in each incision.
Sterilize a jar in a large saucepan of boiling water
for 5 minutes, then place upside down to drain
on a clean tea towel.
Pack the lemons in the jar. They should fit tightly
together. Add the coarse sea salt. Seal the jar and
leave to macerate for 1 month before consuming.
The lemons will keep for several months.

TIP: Try serving the lemons finely diced with
olives and roasted pistachios as a canapé, or cut
them into rounds and simmer in a tagine (North
African stew).

Salted Capers

Preparation time: 45 minutes
+ overnight standing
No cooking required

300 g (10 oz) capers
300 g (10 oz) coarse sea salt
5 peppercorns

Place the capers in a dish and cover with salt.
Mix well to ensure that the capers are thoroughly
coated. Leave overnight.
The next day, sterilize a preserving jar in a large
saucepan of boiling water for 5 minutes, then
place upside down on a clean tea towel to drain.
Place a fine layer of coarse sea salt in the base of
the jar and add the capers. Add the peppercorns.
Seal the jar with an airtight lid and store in a cool,
dark place.

TIP: You can use these capers as and when you
need them, making sure that you rinse them
thoroughly under cold running water first. Uses
include garnishing pizzas, spicing up a veal stew
or pasta salad, or indeed as the essential flavour
in caper sauce.
After opening, store the jar in the refrigerator.

Salted Capers

Olive Fougasse

Add 2 tablespoons of olive oil to
250 g (8 oz) bread dough and knead
in 50 g (2 oz) thinly sliced, pitted Black
Olives (see Tip page 74). Shape into a
rectangle and slash the top 3–4 times.
Bake for about 25 minutes in a
preheated oven 180°C (350°F), Gas
Mark 4.

Anchovy Potatoes

Cook whole, unpeeled potatoes in a
large saucepan of lightly salted,
boiling water with a little thyme and
bay leaves. Drain, peel and halve.
Hollow out the cut sides very slightly
and garnish with Anchovies in Oil (see
page 18) and finely chopped chives.

Smoked Fish Pâté and Caper Savoury

This is a simple recipe for summer starters. Rinse some Salted Capers (see page 74) and pat dry with kitchen paper. Stamp out rounds of bread with a biscuit cutter and spread with ready-made smoked fish pâté. Place 2–3 capers on top.

Cold Meat with Samphire

If you have some left-over cold meat, cut it into slices that are not too thick or dice it up and serve it with samphire, called by some 'the asparagus of the sea'.

Lemon Chicken Tagine

Preparation time: 15 minutes
Cooking time: 2 hours
4–6 servings

1 Moroccan Preserved Lemon (see page 74)
1 tablespoon olive oil
4–6 chicken pieces
2 onions, chopped
½ teaspoon ground cinnamon
2 tablespoons clear honey
250 ml (8 fl oz) chicken stock
salt and pepper
2 tablespoons Tomato Coulis (see page 96),
to serve

Bring a pan of salted water to the boil, add the
lemon and simmer for about 10 minutes. Drain
well and slice.
Heat the oil in a flameproof casserole, add the
chicken pieces and cook, turning frequently, until
browned all over. Remove the chicken from the
casserole and keep warm.
Add the onions to the casserole and cook, stirring
occasionally, for about 5 minutes, until softened.
Return the chicken to the casserole, add the
cinnamon and season with salt and pepper.
Stir in the honey and stock.
Cover and cook in a preheated oven, 120°C
(250°F), Gas Mark ½, for about 1½ hours.
Add the lemon to the casserole, lower the oven
temperature to 110°C (225°F), Gas Mark ¼ and
cook for a further 20 minutes.
Taste and adjust the seasoning, if necessary, and
serve immediately with the tomato coulis.

Lemon Chicken Tagine

speciality
preserves

Confit of Duck

Preparation time: 15 minutes
+ overnight standing
Cooking time: 2¾ hours

1 duck, cut into pieces including the fat
thyme sprigs
1 bay leaf
cooking salt
pepper

Weigh the duck, then place the pieces in a large
dish with the thyme and bay leaf. Add the
cooking salt, allowing about 20 g (¾ oz) salt for
every 500g (1 lb) duck. The following day, remove
the pieces of duck and wipe carefully with a tea
towel or kitchen paper.
Spoon the duck fat from the dish into a large pan
and melt over a low heat. Add the pieces of meat
and cook for about 45 minutes.
Put the duck pieces into preserving jars, and cover
them with the melted duck fat. Seal the jars and
place in a large pan of boiling water. Boil for
about 2 hours, then remove from the pan and
leave to cool.
Keep the confit for 2–3 months before eating.

Confit of Duck

Ratatouille

Preparation time: 30 minutes
Cooking time: 2 hours

about 5 tablespoons olive oil
5 small garlic cloves, chopped
500 g (1 lb) onions, thinly sliced
750 g (1½ lb) tomatoes, skinned, halved
and deseeded
1 handful of basil leaves
3 pinches of thyme leaves
500 g (1 lb) aubergines, sliced
500 g (1 lb) courgettes, sliced
500 g (1 lb) peppers, halved, deseeded and sliced
into fine strips
salt and pepper

Sterilize the preserving jars in a large pan of
boiling water for 10 minutes. Remove and place
upside down on a clean tea towel to drain.
Heat 2 tablespoons of the olive oil in a pan and
add the garlic, onions, tomatoes, basil and thyme.
Cook over a low heat for about 15 minutes, until
the tomatoes are thick and pulpy.
Heat 1 tablespoon of the remaining oil in another
pan. Add the aubergine slices and cook, turning
frequently, until lightly golden. Season lightly with
salt, then remove from the pan and set aside.
Add the courgette slices to the pan, with the
remaining oil, if necessary. Cook over a medium
heat for about 10 minutes, until lightly golden,
then season lightly with salt. Remove the
courgettes from the pan and set aside.
Add the pepper strips to the pan and cook for
about 10 minutes. Season lightly with salt.
Return all the vegetables to the pan, stir in the
tomato mixture, season generously with pepper
and simmer for 35 minutes.
Ladle the ratatouille into the jars, leaving a
2.5–3.5 cm (1–1½ inch) headspace at the top of
each jar. Seal the jars with airtight lids. Place in a
large saucepan, pour in water to cover and bring
to the boil. Boil for 45 minutes.
Leave the jars to cool in the water in the pan,
then store in a dark, dry place.

Ratatouille

Cassoulet

**Preparation time: 30 minutes
+ overnight standing
Cooking time: 2¾ hours**

625 g (1¼ lb) haricot beans, soaked in cold water
overnight and drained
125 g (4 oz) lightly salted belly pork
1 bouquet garni
1 Toulouse sausage or other garlic-flavoured
cooking sausage
1 tablespoon duck fat
3 pieces of Confit of Duck (see page 82)
400 g boned shoulder of lamb, cut into
large cubes
2 onions, chopped
4 garlic cloves, crushed
6 tomatoes, skinned, seeded and finely chopped
salt and pepper

Place the beans, belly pork and bouquet garni in
a large saucepan and pour in water to cover.
Bring to the boil, then lower the heat and simmer
for about 30 minutes.
Add the sausage and cook for a further
20 minutes.
Place the duck fat and pieces of duck in another
pan and cook until golden brown. Then remove
from the pan.
Add the lamb cubes to the pan and cook until
golden brown. Add the onions, garlic and
tomatoes, pour in a little water and cook for
about 15 minutes.
Drain the beans and set aside. Chop the belly
pork and sausage. Discard the bouquet garni.
Pack the beans and all the pieces of meat into
preserving jars. Seal the jars, place in a large
saucepan of boiling water and boil for about
1½ hours.
To serve the cassoulet, tip it into an ovenproof
dish, sprinkle with a layer of breadcrumbs and
heat it in the oven.
You can also add some grilled Toulouse sausages.

Cassoulet

Provençal-style Aubergines

Preparation time: 20 minutes
Cooking time: 1¼ hours
Makes 1 jar (1 litre/1¾ pints)

2 tablespoons olive oil
2 garlic cloves, chopped
2 onions, chopped
1 bunch of parsley, chopped
10 ripe tomatoes, skinned
pinch of sugar
2 teaspoons herbes de Provence
2 aubergines, thickly sliced
2 bay leaves
salt

Sterilize the preserving jar in a large pan of boiling water for 10 minutes, then place upside down on a clean tea towel to drain.
Heat the olive oil in a large saucepan. Add the garlic, onions, parsley, tomatoes, sugar and herbes de Provence, season with salt and cook over a low heat, stirring occasionally, for about 5 minutes, until the onions have softened.
Add the aubergines and bay leaves, then pour in sufficient water to half-fill the pan. Bring to the boil, then simmer for about 1¼ hours, until the vegetables have reduced.
Spoon the mixture into the jar, leaving 2.5–3.5 cm (1–1½ inch) headspace, then seal with an airtight lid.
Place the jar in a large pan, pour in water to cover and bring to the boil. Boil for 1 hour, then leave the jar to cool in the water.
The following day, bring back to the boil for 30 minutes, then leave to cool.
Store the jars in a dark, dry place.

Provençal-style Aubergines

bottled vegetables

Peas and Carrots

Preparation time: 15 minutes
Cooking time: 1¼ hours

750 g (1½ lb) peas, shelled
300 g (10 oz) young carrots, cut into chunks
3 litres (5¼ pints) water
pinch of sugar
salt

Sterilize the preserving jars in a large saucepan of boiling water for 10 minutes, then remove the jars and place upside down on a clean tea towel to drain.

Bring a large saucepan of lightly salted water to the boil. Add the peas and blanch for 3 minutes. Drain, rinse under cold running water, then drain again.

Pack the peas into the jars and place the carrots on top.

Bring the measured water to the boil, add 15 g (½ oz) salt and stir until dissolved.

Pour the salted water into the jars, leaving a 2.5–3.5 cm (1–1½ inch) headspace. Add the pinch of sugar.

Seal the jars with airtight lids. Place in a large saucepan, add water to cover and bring to the boil. Boil for 1 hour, then leave to cool in the water in the saucepan.

Store in a dark, dry place.

Asparagus

Preparation time: 15 minutes
Cooking time: 1½ hours

750 g (1½ lb) short asparagus spears of about equal thickness, peeled if necessary
3 litres (5¼ pints) water
salt

Sterilize the preserving jars in a large saucepan of boiling water for 10 minutes, then remove and place upside down on a clean tea towel to drain. Tie the asparagus spears in bunches of 10 using fine string. Bring a large saucepan of lightly salted water to the boil and add the asparagus bunches. Blanch for 3 minutes. Drain, rinse under cold running water and drain again.

Untie the bundles and pack the asparagus into the jars, with the tips uppermost.

Bring the measured water to the boil, add 15 g (½ oz) salt and stir until dissolved.

Pour the salted water into the jars to cover the asparagus, leaving a 2.5–3.5 cm (1–1½ inch) headspace at the top. Seal with airtight lids.

Place the jars in a large saucepan, add water to cover and bring to the boil. Boil for 1 hour, then leave to cool in the saucepan of water.

Next day, bring back to the boil and boil for 30 minutes. Leave the jars to cool in the saucepan of water.

Remove when cool and store in a dark, dry place.

French Beans

Preparation time: 15 minutes
Cooking time: 1¼ hours

750 g (1½ lb) French beans, trimmed
3 litres (5¼ pints) water
salt

Sterilize the preserving jars in a large saucepan of boiling water for 10 minutes, then remove and place upside down on a clean tea towel to drain.
Bring a large saucepan of lightly salted water to the boil and add the beans. Blanch them for 3 minutes, then drain and rinse under cold running water. Drain again and pack the beans in the jars.
Bring the measured water to the boil, add 15 g (½ oz) salt and stir until dissolved.
Pour the salted water into the jars to cover the beans, leaving a 2.5–3.5 cm (1–1½ inch) headspace, and seal the jars with airtight lids.
Place the jars in a large saucepan, add water to cover and bring to the boil. Boil for 1¼ hours, then leave the jars to cool in the water in the pan. Store in a dark, dry place.

Celery

Preparation time: 15 minutes
Cooking time: 1¼ hours

750 g (1½ lb) celery, trimmed
3 litres (5¼ pints) water
salt

Sterilize the preserving jars in a large saucepan of boiling water for 10 minutes, then remove and place upside down on a clean tea towel to drain. Divide the celery into sections.
Bring a large saucepan of lightly salted water to the boil and add the celery. Blanch for 3 minutes, then drain and rinse under cold running water. Drain again and pack into the jars.
Bring the measured water to the boil, add 15 g (½ oz) salt and stir until dissolved.
Pour the salted water into the jars to cover the celery, leaving a 2.5–3.5 cm (1–1½ inch) headspace, and seal the jars with airtight lids.
Place the jars in a large saucepan, add water to cover and bring to the boil. Boil for 1¼ hours, then leave the jars to cool in the water in the pan. Store in a dark, dry place.

French Beans

Tomato Coulis

Preparation time: 15 minutes
Cooking time: 2¼ hours

2 kg (4 lb) ripe beef tomatoes, skinned,
quartered and deseeded
6 tablespoons olive oil
3 garlic cloves, crushed
1 teaspoon granulated or caster sugar
1 small bay leaf
2 tablespoons chopped fresh parsley
1 thyme sprig
4 basil leaves
salt and pepper

Sterilize the preserving jars in a large saucepan
of boiling water for 10 minutes, then remove and
place upside down on a clean tea towel to drain.
Cut the tomato quarters into large pieces.
Heat the olive oil in a deep pan, add the garlic
and cook over a very low heat for 3 minutes.
Add the tomatoes, sugar, bay leaf, parsley, thyme,
and basil. Season with salt and pepper and stir
well. Cover and cook over a low heat for about
30 minutes.
Remove and discard the bay leaf and thyme. Pour
the tomato mixture into a food processor or
blender and process to a smooth purée.
Ladle the tomato coulis into the jars and seal with
airtight lids.
Place the jars in a large saucepan, add water to
cover and bring to the boil. Boil for 1¼ hours.
Leave the jars to cool in the water in the pan.
Store in a dark, dry place.

TIP: This tomato coulis is a perfect garnish for
pizza, rice or meatballs.

Chard

Preparation time: 15 minutes
Cooking time: 1¼ hours

750 g (1 lb) chard, white stems only
3 litres (5¼ pints) water
salt

Sterilize the preserving jars in a large saucepan of
boiling water for 10 minutes, then remove and
place upside down on a clean tea towel to drain.
Remove any stringy parts from the chard and cut
the stems into 2.5 cm (1 inch) lengths. Bring a
large saucepan of lightly salted water to the boil
and add the chard. Blanch for 3 minutes, then
drain and rinse under cold running water. Drain
well again and pack into the jars.
Bring the measured water to the boil, add 15 g
(½ oz) salt and stir until dissolved.
Pour the salted water into the jars to cover the
chard, leaving a 2.5–3.5 cm (1–1½ inch)
headspace, and seal with airtight lids.
Place the jars in a large saucepan, add water to
cover and bring to the boil. Boil for 1¼ hours,
then leave the jars to cool completely in the water
in the saucepan.
Store in a dark, dry place.

Tomato Coulis

Tagliatelle with Mushrooms and Basil

Preparation time: 15 minutes
Cooking time: 20 minutes
4 servings

2 tablespoons olive oil, plus extra to serve
1 shallot, thinly sliced
250 g (8 oz) Bottled Mushrooms
(see right), drained
400 g (13 oz) dried tagliatelle
40 basil leaves, finely chopped
coarse sea salt and pepper

Heat the olive oil in a large frying pan, add the shallot and cook over a low heat until golden. Add the mushrooms and cook for 2–3 minutes to release their flavour. Remove from the heat and keep warm.
Bring 6 litres (10½ pints) water to the boil in a large pan. Add 3 tablespoons sea salt and the tagliatelle, bring back to the boil and cook for 8–10 minutes, until tender but still firm to the bite. Drain and add to the frying pan. Return the frying pan to the heat and toss the mixture quickly, adding the chopped basil.
Serve with a little extra olive oil and pepper.

Bottled Mushrooms

Preparation time: 20 minutes + cooling
Cooking time: 1¼ hours

2–3 kg (4–6 lb) wild or mixed wild and cultivated mushrooms
250 ml (8 fl oz) white wine
1 onion, cut into quarters
2–3 garlic cloves
bouquet garni, made from thyme, bay and savory
salt and pepper

Sterilize the preserving jars in a large saucepan of boiling water for 10 minutes, then remove and place upside down on a clean tea towel to drain. Cut any large mushrooms into halves or quarters. Blanch in a pan of boiling water for 2–3 minutes, then drain.
Pour 750 ml (1¼ pints) water into a large pan, add the wine, onion, garlic and the bouquet garni and season with salt and plenty of pepper. Bring to the boil, add the mushrooms and cook, stirring occasionally, for a further 10 minutes.
Leave the mushrooms to cool in the cooking liquid, then remove with a slotted spoon, drain well and pat dry. Strain the cooking liquid into a jug. Discard the contents of the strainer.
Pack the mushrooms into the jars. Pour the cooking liquid into the jars to cover the mushrooms, leaving a 2.5–3.5 cm (1–1½ inch) headspace and seal the jars with airtight lids. Place the jars in a large saucepan, add water to cover and bring to the boil. Boil for 1 hour, then leave the jars to cool in the water in the pan. Store in a dark, dry place.

Bottled Mushrooms

fruit preserves

Strawberry Jam

**Preparation time: 10 minutes
+ overnight standing
Cooking time: 20 minutes
Makes 6 jars (250 g/8 oz each)**

1 kg (2 lb) strawberries, hulled
875 g (1¾ lb) granulated sugar
4 tablespoons lemon juice

Place all the ingredients in a dish, cover and leave to stand overnight in a cool place. The following day, prepare the jars according to the instructions at the bottom of the page.
Strain the strawberries, reserving the juice. Pour the juice into a preserving pan.
Bring to the boil, stirring constantly with a wooden spoon. Add the strawberries and boil for about 5 minutes. Strain the strawberries, return the sugary juice to the pan and reduce over a medium heat for 5 minutes. Return the strawberries to the pan, bring back to the boil and boil for 5 minutes.
Gently stir with the wooden spoon, then use a skimmer or slotted spoon to remove the scum that has formed on the surface.
Ladle the jam into the jars while still hot and seal according to the instructions at the bottom of the page.

Damson Jam

**Preparation time: 15 minutes
Cooking time: 20 minutes
Makes 6 jars (250 g/8 oz each)**

750 g (1½ lb) granulated sugar
125 ml (4 fl oz) water
1 kg (2 lb) damsons, halved and pitted
100 g (3½ oz) blanched almonds

Prepare the jars according to the instructions at the bottom of the page.
Put the sugar into a preserving pan and pour in the water. Bring to the boil, stirring constantly, then add the damsons and cook over a medium heat, stirring frequently, for about 20 minutes. Using a skimmer or slotted spoon, remove the scum that has formed on the surface. Stir in the almonds.
Ladle the jam into the jars while still hot and seal according to the instructions at the bottom of the page.

Apricot Jam

**Preparation time: 10 minutes
+ overnight standing
Cooking time: 20 minutes
Makes 4 jars (250 g/8 oz each)**

625 g (1¼ lb) ripe, firm apricots, halved and pitted
400 g (13 oz) granulated sugar
2 tablespoons lemon juice

Place all the ingredients in a large dish, cover and leave to stand overnight in a cool place. The following day, prepare the jars according to the instructions at the bottom of the page.
Put the apricots, sugar and lemon juice into a preserving pan. Bring to the boil over a high heat, stirring constantly with a wooden spoon. Lower the heat to medium and cook for about 20 minutes. Stir with the wooden spoon, then use a skimmer or slotted spoon to remove the scum that has formed on the surface.
Ladle the jam into the jars while still hot and seal according to the instructions at the bottom of the page.

Raspberry Jam

**Preparation time: 10 minutes
Cooking time: 25 minutes
Makes 6 jars (250 g/8 oz each)**

1 kg (2 lb) raspberries
750 g (1½ lb) granulated sugar
4 tablespoons lemon

Prepare the jars according to the instructions at the bottom of the page.
Put the raspberries, sugar and lemon juice into a preserving pan and bring to the boil over a fairly high heat, stirring constantly with a wooden spoon. Use a skimmer or slotted spoon to remove the scum that has formed on the surface.
Ladle the jam into the jars while still hot and seal according to the instructions at the bottom of the page.

Preparing the jars

Place the jars in a preheated oven, 110°C (225°F), Gas Mark ¼, for 5 minutes. Remove from the oven and leave to cool on a clean tea towel.

Potting the jam

Using a small ladle, fill the jars with jam to the top. Carefully wipe off any spills on the outside of the jars, then seal with airtight lids and turn the jars upside down. Leave to cool, then store in a dark, dry place.

Rhubarb Jam

**Preparation time: 10 minutes
+ overnight standing
Cooking time: 20 minutes
Makes 7 jars (250 g/8 oz each)**

1 kg (2 lb) rhubarb, cut into short lengths
1 kg (2 lb) granulated sugar
1 unwaxed orange, sliced (optional)

Put the rhubarb and the sugar into a large dish,
cover and leave to stand overnight in a cool place.
The following day, prepare the jars according to
the instructions at the bottom of the page. Strain
the rhubarb, reserving the juice, and set aside.
Pour the juice into a preserving pan and bring to
the boil over a high heat. Boil for 1–2 minutes,
then add the rhubarb. Lower the heat and
simmer, stirring frequently with a wooden spoon.
Using a skimmer or slotted spoon, remove the
scum that has formed on the surface.
If you like, add the orange slices.
Ladle the jam into the jars while still hot and seal
according to the instructions at the bottom of
the page.

Plum Jam

**Preparation time: 10 minutes
+ overnight standing
Cooking time: 20 minutes
Makes 7 jars (250 g each)**

1 kg (2 lb) quetsch or other cooking plums,
halved and pitted
875 kg (1¾ lb) granulated sugar
4 tablespoons lemon juice

Put all the ingredients into a large dish, cover and
leave to stand overnight in a cool place.
The following day, prepare the jars according to
the instructions at the bottom of the page.
Put the plums, sugar and lemon juice into a
preserving pan and bring to the boil over a high
heat, stirring constantly with a wooden spoon.
Remove the scum that has formed on the surface.
Ladle the jam into the jars while still hot and seal
according to the instructions at the bottom of
the page.

Seville Orange Marmalade

**Preparation time: 25 minutes
Cooking time: 1 hour
Makes 7 jars (250 g/8 oz each)**

15 unwaxed Seville oranges
1 kg (2 lb) granulated sugar
4 tablespoons lemon juice

Prepare the jars according to the instructions at
the bottom of the page.
Use a vegetable peeler to remove the rind from
3 of the oranges. Cut the rind into fine strips
about 2.5 cm (1 inch) long. Put the strips of rind
into a saucepan, add water to cover and bring to
the boil. Lower the heat and simmer until the rind
feels tender to the touch.
Squeeze all the oranges. Put the orange juice,
sugar and lemon juice into a preserving pan and
cook over a medium heat for about 40 minutes,
stirring the liquid with a wooden spoon. Add the
orange rind, and cook for about 20 minutes.
Using a skimmer or slotted spoon, remove the
scum that has formed on the surface.
Ladle the marmalade into the jars while still hot
and seal according to the instructions at the
bottom of the page.

Melon Jam

**Preparation time: 25 minutes + 2 hours standing
Cooking time: 50 minutes
Makes 6 jars (250 g/8 oz each)**

2 melons, halved, deseeded, peeled and diced
750 g (1½ lb) granulated sugar per 1 kg (2 lb)
of melon flesh
8 tablespoons lemon juice
a few blanched almonds

Prepare the jars according to the instructions at
the bottom of the page.
If the flesh from near the melon rinds seems hard,
blanch it in boiling water for 2 minutes.
Place the melon in a dish with the sugar and
lemon juice. Leave to stand for 2 hours.
Pour the contents of the dish into a preserving
pan and cook over a medium heat for about
50 minutes, stirring with a wooden spoon.
Using a skimmer or slotted spoon, remove the
scum that has formed on the surface.
Stir in the almonds.
Ladle the jam into the jars while still hot and seal
according to the instructions at the bottom of
the page.

Preparing the jars

Place the jars in a preheated oven, 110°C (225°F), Gas Mark ¼, for 5 minutes. Remove from the oven and
leave to cool on a clean tea towel.

Potting the jam

Using a small ladle, fill the jars with jam to the top. Carefully wipe off any spills on the outside of the jars,
then seal with airtight lids and turn the jars upside down. Leave to cool, then store in a dark, dry place.

Chestnut Jam

Preparation time: 25 minutes
Cooking time: 35 minutes
Makes 6 jars (250 g/8 oz each)

1 kg (2 lb) chestnuts
750 g (1½ lb) granulated sugar
1 vanilla pod

Prepare the jars according to the instructions at the bottom of the page.
Cut into the chestnuts using a small, pointed knife. Bring a large pan of water to the boil, add the chestnuts, then drain. Remove both the shells and their inner skins with the blade of a knife. Bring another pan of water to the boil and add the peeled chestnuts. Simmer gently for about 15 minutes, then remove the chestnuts from the pan with a slotted spoon and crush with the back of a spoon. Alternatively push them through a food mill.
Pour the chestnut cooking water into a preserving pan and add the sugar. Heat gently, stirring continuously. As soon as the liquid starts to boil, add the chestnuts and vanilla pod and cook over a medium heat, stirring frequently, for about 20 minutes.
Remove the vanilla pod.
Ladle the jam into the jars while still hot according to the instructions at the bottom of the page. Cut the vanilla pod into small pieces and add a piece to each jar, then seal.

Mirabelle Plum Jam

Preparation time: 10 minutes
+ overnight standing
Cooking time: 30 minutes
Makes 6 jars (250 g/8 oz each)

1 kg (2 lb) mirabelle or cherry plums
(or small plums), halved and pitted
875 kg (1¾ lb) granulated sugar
4 tablespoons lemon juice

Put all the ingredients into a large dish, cover and leave to stand overnight in a cool place.
The following day, prepare the jars according to the instructions at the bottom of the page.
Put the plums, sugar and lemon juice into a preserving pan and bring to the boil over a high heat, stirring constantly with a wooden spoon.
Cook for about 30 minutes, then using a skimmer or slotted spoon, to remove the scum that has formed on the surface.
Ladle the jam into the jars while still hot and seal according to the instructions at the bottom of the page.

Preparing the jars

Place the jars in a preheated oven, 110°C (225°F), Gas Mark ¼, for 5 minutes. Remove from the oven and leave to cool on a clean tea towel.

Potting the jam

Using a small ladle, fill the jars with jam to the top. Carefully wipe off any spills on the outside of the jars, then seal with airtight lids and turn the jars upside down. Leave to cool, then store in a dark, dry place.

Chestnut Jam

Blackcurrant Jelly

Preparation time: 20 minutes
Cooking time: 35 minutes
Makes 5–6 jars (250 g/8 oz each)

1.5 kg (3 lb) blackcurrants
125 ml (4 fl oz) water
1 kg (2 lb) granulated sugar
4 tablespoons lemon juice

Prepare the jars according to the instructions at the bottom of the page.

Put the blackcurrants into a large, heavy-based saucepan, pour in the water and heat gently until the berries have burst. Place the fruit in a muslin bag or wrap in a square of muslin and squeeze hard over a large bowl to remove as much juice as possible. Discard the blackcurrant pulp.

Pour the juice into a preserving pan and add the sugar and lemon juice. Cook over a medium heat for about 15 minutes.

Ladle the jelly into the jars while still hot and seal according to the instructions at the bottom of the page. Leave to cool, then store in a dark, dry place.

Redcurrant Jelly

Preparation time: 15 minutes
Cooking time: 15 minutes
Makes 5–6 jars (250 g/8 oz each)

1.5 kg (3 lb) redcurrants
1 kg (2 lb) granulated sugar
4 tablespoons lemon juice

Prepare the jars according to the instructions at the bottom of the page.

Place the redcurrants in a muslin bag or wrap in a square of muslin and squeeze hard over a large bowl to remove as much juice as possible. Discard the redcurrant pulp.

Pour the juice into a preserving pan and add the sugar and lemon juice. Cook over a medium heat for about 15 minutes.

Ladle into the jars and seal according to the instructions at the bottom of the page, then leave them to cool and store in a dark, dry place.

TIP: You do not need to cook the redcurrants in advance, as you do for blackberries and blackcurrants. Redcurrant jelly sets very easily. In the past people even used to make redcurrant jelly with no cooking at all.

Preparing the jars

Place the jars in a preheated oven, 110°C (225°F), Gas Mark ¼, for 5 minutes. Remove from the oven and leave to cool on a clean tea towel.

Potting the jam

Using a small ladle, fill the jars with jam to the top. Carefully wipe off any spills on the outside of the jars, then seal with airtight lids and turn the jars upside down. Leave to cool, then store in a dark, dry place.

Blackcurrant Jelly

White Wine Jelly

Preparation time: 25 minutes
Cooking time: 25 minutes
Makes 5 jars (250 g/8 oz each)

1 bottle medium dry white wine
500 ml (17 fl oz) apple juice
750 g (1½ lb) granulated sugar

Prepare the jars according to the instructions at the bottom of the page.
Pour the wine into a preserving pan and bring to the boil. Remove from the heat and briefly flambé the contents of the pan.
Pour in the apple juice and granulated sugar, stir with a wooden spoon and return to the heat. Cook over a fairly high heat, stirring frequently, for 15 minutes. Use a skimmer or slotted spoon to remove the scum that has formed on the surface.
Ladle the jelly into the jars while still hot and seal according to the instructions at the bottom of the page. Leave them to cool, then store them in a dark, dry place.

TIP: This jelly is delicious with cold roast pork.

Preparing the jars

Place the jars in a preheated oven, 110°C (225°F), Gas Mark ¼, for 5 minutes. Remove from the oven and leave to cool on a clean tea towel.

Potting the jam

Using a small ladle, fill the jars with jam to the top. Carefully wipe off any spills on the outside of the jars, then seal with airtight lids and turn the jars upside down. Leave to cool, then store in a dark, dry place.

White Wine Jelly

Apple and Quince Compote

Preparation time: 15 minutes + cooling + chilling
Cooking time: 50 minutes

2 ripe quinces, peeled, quartered and cored
4 apples, peeled, quartered and cored
150 g (5 oz) caster sugar
1 vanilla pod
125 ml (4 fl oz) water

Put all the ingredients into a large saucepan, bring to the boil, then cover and simmer, stirring frequently, for about 50 minutes. If necessary, add a little more water to prevent the mixture from sticking to the base of the pan.
Leave the compote to cool, then chill in the refrigerator before serving.

TIP: Quinces are not widely available, but they are sometimes on sale in the late autumn. If you can't find them, use pears instead.

Spicy Pear Compote

Preparation time: 15 minutes + cooling + chilling
Cooking time: 50 minutes

1.25 kg (2½ lb) pears, peeled, quartered and cored
150 g (5 oz) brown sugar
¼ teaspoon ground ginger
¼ teaspoon ground cinnamon
1 vanilla pod
125 ml (4 fl oz) water

Put all the ingredients into a large saucepan, bring to the boil, then cover and simmer over a low heat for about 50 minutes.
Leave the compote to cool, then chill in the refrigerator. Serve with a little crème fraîche.

Compotes as preserves

To preserve compotes, reduce the cooking time for the fruit to 35 minutes. Prepare your jars as for jam. Ladle the hot compote into the jars, seal and sterilize for 20 minutes in a large pan of boiling water. Leave them to cool before storing in a dark, dry place.

Spicy Pear Compote and Apple and Quince Compote

Crystallized Quince

Preparation time: 15 minutes + 3 days drying
Cooking time: 35 minutes

625 g (1¼ lb) ripe quinces, quartered
250 ml (8 fl oz) water
about 500 g (1 lb) granulated sugar
caster sugar, for dusting

Put the quinces in a preserving pan, add the water, and bring to the boil. Lower the heat and simmer for about 15 minutes, until tender.
Drain, peel and core then push the pieces of quince through a food mill on the finest setting. Alternatively, process in a food processor or blender to a purée
Weigh the purée, then return it to the preserving pan with the same weight of sugar and bring to the boil. Simmer gently, stirring constantly, for 20 minutes, until the mixture forms a thick paste.
Spoon the paste on to a baking sheet lined with greaseproof paper and spread to an even depth of about 2.5 cm (1 inch).
Leave to dry in a cool, dry place for 3 days, then stamp out shapes with a biscuit cutter.
Dust the shapes with caster sugar and arrange them in an airtight container lined with a sheet of greaseproof paper.

TIP: Apples or pears can be used instead of quinces.

Crystallized Quince

Pears in Syrup

Preparation time: 15 minutes
Cooking time: 15 minutes

For each 1-litre (1¾ pint) jar:
1.25 kg (2½ lb) ripe, slightly firm pears, peeled, quartered and cored
2 tablespoons caster sugar
4 tablespoons lemon juice

Sterilize the preserving jars in a large pan of boiling water for 10 minutes, then place upside down on a clean tea towel to drain.
Pack the pears into the dry jars, sprinkle with caster sugar and pour in the lemon juice.
Seal the jars with airtight lids and place in a large saucepan. Add water to cover and bring to the boil. Boil for about 15 minutes.
Leave the jars to cool in the water, then store in a cool, dark place.

Wild Blackberries in Syrup

Preparation time: 15 minutes
Cooking time: 15 minutes

For each 1-litre (1¾ pint) jar:
1 kg (2 lb) wild blackberries
2 tablespoons caster sugar
4 tablespoons lemon juice

Sterilize the preserving jars in a large pan of boiling water for 10 minutes, then place upside on a clean tea towel to drain dry.
Pack the blackberries into the dry jars, sprinkle with caster sugar, then pour in the lemon juice.
Seal the jars with airtight lids and place them in a large pan. Add water to cover and bring to the boil. Boil for about 15 minutes.
Leave the jars to cool in the pan of water, then store in a cool, dark place.

TIP: Wild blackberries grow copiously in hedgerows and woodlands and can be picked from July onwards. They are very succulent with a sharp, yet sweet flavour. Cultivated blackberries are almost as delicious, are widely available from all supermarkets and may be substituted for wild.

Pears in Syrup

Plums in Syrup

Preparation time: 15 minutes
Cooking time: 15 minutes

For each 1-litre (1¾ pint) jar:
1 kg (2 lb) ripe, slightly firm plums
2 tablespoons caster sugar
4 tablespoons lemon juice

Sterilize the preserving jars in a large pan of boiling water for 10 minutes, then place upside down on a clean tea towel to drain.
Pack the plums into the dry jars, then add the sugar and the lemon juice.
Seal the jars with airtight lids and place them in a large saucepan. Add water to cover and bring to the boil. Boil for about 15 minutes.
Leave the jars to cool in the water, then store them in a cool, dark place.

Cherries in Syrup

Preparation time: 15 minutes
Cooking time: 15 minutes

For each 1-litre (1¾ pint) jar:
1 kg (2 lb) ripe, slightly firm cherries
2 tablespoons caster sugar
4 tablespoons lemon juice

Sterilize the preserving jars in a large pan of boiling water for 10 minutes, then place upside down on a clean tea towel to drain.
Pit 4–5 of the cherries, wrap the pits in a tea towel and hit them with a hammer.
Pack the cherries into the dry jars, add the broken pieces of cherry pit and the sugar and pour in the lemon juice.
Seal the jars with airtight lids and place them in a large saucepan. Add water to cover and bring to the boil. Boil for about 15 minutes.
Leave the jars to cool in the water, then store them in a cool, dark place.

Plums in Syrup

Vanilla Apricots

Preparation time: 15 minutes
Cooking time: 15 minutes

For each 1-litre (1¾ pint) jar:
1.25 kg (2½ lb) ripe, slightly firm apricots,
halved and pitted, with 4–5 pits reserved
1 vanilla pod
2 tablespoons caster sugar
4 tablespoons lemon juice

Sterilize the preserving jars in a large pan of
boiling water for 10 minutes, then place upside
down on a clean tea towel to drain.
Wrap the reserved apricot pits in a tea towel and
hit them with a hammer.
Pack the apricot halves into the dry jars with the
broken pieces of pit and the vanilla pod, then add
the sugar and lemon juice.
Seal the jars with airtight lids and place them in a
large saucepan. Add water to cover and bring to
the boil. Boil for about 15 minutes.
Leave the jars to cool in the water, then store
them in a cool, dark place.

Clementines in Syrup

Preparation time: 15 minutes
Cooking time: 1 hour

1 kg (2 lb) unwaxed clementines
250 g (8 oz) caster sugar
1 litre (1¾ pints) water

Sterilize the preserving jars in a large pan of
boiling water for 10 minutes, then place upside
down on a clean tea towel to drain.
Place the clementines in a saucepan of cold water.
Bring to the boil, then reduce the heat and
simmer for about 12 minutes. Remove the fruit
and drain well.
Put the sugar into a heavy-based saucepan, pour
in the measured water and heat gently, stirring
until the sugar has dissolved. Bring to the boil,
then add the clementines, lower the heat and
simmer for about 30 minutes.
Remove the pan from the heat and lift out the
clementines with a slotted spoon. Pack the
clementines into the jars and pour in the syrup.
Seal the jars with airtight lids and place them in a
large saucepan. Add water to cover and bring to
the boil. Boil for about 15 minutes.
Leave the jars to cool in the water, then store
them in a cool, dark place.

TIP: You will find that these clementines are
delicious with natural yogurt. The syrup will add
a delicate flavour to fresh fruit salad.

Clementines in Syrup

Vanilla Sugar

Preparation time: 5 minutes
No cooking required

1 vanilla pod
1 kg (2 lb) caster sugar

Slit the vanilla pod lengthways using a small
pointed knife. Scrape out the inside and remove
and reserve the seeds.
Bury the vanilla pod in the sugar in a jar and stir
in the seeds until evenly distributed.
Leave for 2–3 days before using.

TIP: This vanilla sugar is delicious in fruit salad.
You can also use it to flavour cakes.

Star Anise Sugar

Preparation time: 5 minutes
No cooking required

2 star anise
1 kg (2 lb) caster sugar

Add the star anise to the sugar in a jar and stir
occasionally to mix.
Leave for 2–3 days before using.

TIP: This sugar is ideal for flavouring fruit salad.
You can also make it with brown sugar (as
illustrated opposite).

Cinnamon Sugar

Preparation time: 5 minutes
No cooking required

2 cinnamon sticks
1 kg (2 lb) soft brown sugar

Bury the cinnamon sticks in the brown sugar in a
jar. Stir occasionally.
Leave for 2–3 days before using.

TIP: This cinnamon sugar is a delicious flavouring
for hot chocolate, apple tarts and crumbles.

Star Anise Sugar and Vanilla Sugar

Glazed Fruit Tart

This is a good way to give a professional touch to any fruit tart. Mix some fruit jelly, such as Redcurrant Jelly (see page 108) with a little water and a dash of liqueur, such as kirsch or amaretto, in a saucepan. Heat gently, stirring until the jelly has dissolved. Bake the pastry case blind, then spread a thin layer of the mixture over the base. Arrange the fruit on top, then brush with the remainder of the jelly mixture. You will find that this greatly enhances both the flavour and appearance of your tart.

Chocolate Sponges with Clementines in Syrup

Grease 6 ramekins with butter and lightly sprinkle with flour. Place 250 g (8 oz) chocolate, broken into pieces, and 250 g (8 oz) diced butter in a heatproof bowl and melt over a pan of barely simmering water. Beat 8 egg yolks with 200 g (7 oz) brown sugar until the mixture is pale and fluffy. Stir in the chocolate mixture. Beat 4 egg whites until stiff and fold into the mixture. Spoon the mixture into the ramekins so that they are about two-thirds full. Bake in a preheated oven,150°C (300°F), Gas Mark 2, for 30 minutes. About 5 minutes before the end of the cooking time, place sliced Clementines in Syrup (see page 120) on top of each ramekin. Serve warm.

Cheese and Crystallized Quince

Crystallized Quince (see page 114) can be eaten just as it comes, but it is also great served with cheese.

Brioche and Damson Jam

As a tea-time treat for children, cut the tops off individual brioches, hollow them out slightly and spread with a home-made preserve such as Damson Jam (see page 102).

Scones with Apricot Jam

The sweet, smooth taste of scones is even more delicious when combined with the tart flavour of Apricot Jam (see page 102). Remember to warm the scones in the oven for a few minutes before you serve them.

Linzertorte

**Preparation time: 20 minutes
+ 1 hour resting + cooling
Cooking time: 30 minutes
4–6 servings**

125 g (4 oz) plain flour
1 egg, lightly beaten
125 g (4oz) butter, diced (at room temperature)
125 g (4 oz) caster sugar
125 g (4 oz) ground almonds
grated rind of ¼ unwaxed lemon
1 teaspoon ground cinnamon
1 teaspoon cocoa powder
150 g (5 oz) Raspberry Jam (see page 102)
250 ml (8 fl oz) milk
salt

Sift the flour on to a work surface and make a
well in the centre. Put the egg, butter, sugar and
a pinch of salt into the well. Mix lightly with your
fingertips, then add the almonds, lemon rind,
cinnamon and cocoa powder. Gradually
incorporate the flour with your fingertips. Lightly
knead the dough, roll it into a ball, wrap in
clingfilm and leave to rest in the refrigerator for at
least 1 hour.
Roll out two-thirds of the dough into a round and
use to line a 25 cm (10 inch) round or square flan
dish. Spread the jam evenly over the pastry base.
Roll out the remaining dough, and cut it into
1 cm (½ inch wide) strips . Arrange these strips in
a criss-cross pattern over the jam and brush with
a little milk. Bake in a preheated oven 180°C
(350°F), Gas Mark 4, for 30 minutes. Leave to
cool before serving.

TIP: The tart is best served with whipped cream.
Your pastry will be even better if you make it
the day before.

Linzertorte

drying

Drying herbs is the best way to retain their aroma. You can use them all year round to prepare herbal teas as well as for cooking. This very simple technique is also useful for preserving medicinal herbs.

A word of advice

Herbs are best picked in the early morning and in dry weather. The ideal time is just after the dew has disappeared, but before the sun becomes hot, because the heat evaporates the plants' essential oils. Avoid harvesting in the rain.

Dry your herbs by spreading them out on a tray in a single layer without overlapping.

They are best stored in a dark, dry place. A jar in a cupboard or an airtight container will do.

Bay

Preparation time: 10 minutes + drying
No cooking required
Using secateurs, carefully remove leaves from the tree. Do not use spotted or damaged leaves. Spread out the leaves in a dry place for a few days, turning them over occasionally, then store in an airtight container.

Thyme

Preparation time: 10 minutes + drying
No cooking required
Use secateurs to cut some sprigs. Spread them out on a tray in a dry place and leave for a few days, turning them over occasionally. Then store in an airtight container.

TIP: A tea made from thyme is reputed to be excellent for colds – and in the kitchen it is a little marvel.

Rosemary

Preparation time: 10 minutes + drying
No cooking required
Remove several small branches using secateurs. Spread them out on a tray in a dry place for a few days, turning them over occasionally, then store in an airtight container.

TIP: Rosemary is a very aromatic plant which subtly flavours meats and grilled fish. It is also widely used in Mediterranean recipes.

Rosemary

Lemon Verbena

Preparation time: 10 minutes + drying
No cooking required

Pick the verbena leaves. Spread them out on a tray and leave in a dry place, turning them over occasionally. Leave for about 2 weeks before using them to make tea. Verbena is said to be good for the digestion.
Store in an airtight container.

Cherry Stalks

Preparation time: 10 minutes + drying
No cooking required

Remove the stalks from freshly picked cherries. Spread them out on a tray in a dry place, turning them over occasionally. Leave for about 2 weeks before using them in tea.
This tea has diuretic properties.
Store in an airtight container

Mallow

Preparation time: 10 minutes + drying
No cooking required

Collect some mallow flowers. Spread them out on a tray in a dry place, turning them over occasionally. Leave for about 2 weeks before using them in tisanes.
Store in an airtight container.

Orange Leaves

Preparation time: 10 minutes + drying
No cooking required

Collect some orange leaves. Spread them out on a tray in a dry place, turning them over occasionally. Leave for about 2 weeks before using them. Orange leaves are excellent for making a tea for drinking in the evening, as they have calming properties.
Store in an airtight container.

Camomile Flowers

Preparation time: 10 minutes + drying
No cooking required

Pick some camomile flowers, taking care to cut them off at the very ends of the stalks.
Spread them out on a tray in a dry place, turning them over occasionally. Leave for about 2 weeks before using. Camomile tea is said to aid the digestion.
Store in an airtight container.

Linden Blossom

Preparation time: 10 minutes + drying
No cooking required

First pick the linden blossom – the trees are sometimes known as lime trees, although they are nothing to do with the citrus fruit trees. Spread out the flowers on a tray in a dry place, turning them over occasionally. Leave for about 2 weeks before using them.
Linden flower tea is reputed to have calming properties.
Store in an airtight container.

Dried Apples

Preparation time: 15 minutes
Cooking time: 6–9 hours

2 tablespoons lemon juice
1 kg (2 lb) apples, peeled, cored and sliced
into rings

Half fill a bowl with cold water and stir in the
lemon juice. Add the apple slices and set aside for
10 minutes.
Drain the slices and pat dry. Arrange them on a
tray and place in a preheated oven on its lowest
temperature setting for about 3 hours. Leave the
oven door slightly ajar and occasionally turn the
slices over.
Heat again for 3 hours the next day and a third
time if necessary.
Store the fruit in an airtight container.

Dried Pears

Preparation time: 15 minutes
Cooking time: 6–9 hours

1 kg (2 lb) pears, peeled, halved and cored

Pat the pears dry with kitchen paper and place on
a tray. Place in a preheated oven on its lowest
temperature setting for about 3 hours. Leave the
oven door slightly ajar and turn the pear halves
over occasionally.
Heat again for 3 hours the next day and a third
time if necessary.
Store the fruit in an airtight container.

Dried Apricots

Preparation time: 15 minutes
Cooking time: 6–9 hours

1 kg (2 lb) apricots, halved and pitted

Arrange the apricot halves on an baking sheet
and place in a preheated oven at its lowest
temperature setting for 3 hours. Leave the oven
door slightly ajar and occasionally turn the
apricots over.
Heat again for 3 hours the next day and a third
time if necessary.
Store the fruit in an airtight container.

Dried Pears

Fruit and Chocolate Biscuits

Dice small some Dried Pears, Dried Apples and Dried Apricots (see page 134). Use them instead of – or in addition to – more traditional fruit (like raisins and figs) and nuts (like almonds and hazelnuts) when decorating chocolate biscuits.

Cherry-stalk Tea

Dried Cherry Stalks (see page 132) are renowned for their diuretic qualities, and are ideal for a little 'detox'. To prepare a tea, boil the stalks in water for 1 minute, then cover and leave to infuse.

Camomile Tea

Problems with your digestion? Try a good cup of tea made with dried Camomile Flowers (see page 132). The taste is bitter, but the effect is dramatic. You can also use an infusion of camomile as a mouthwash.

Lemon Verbena Ice Cream

You can make a delicious ice cream by adding 5 tablespoons Lemon Verbena Liqueur (see right) to custard into which you have folded whipped cream. Leave for at least 1 hour in the freezer until set.

Lemon Verbena Liqueur

Put a handful of lemon verbena leaves in a jar with 1 litre (1¾ pints) eau de vie (colourless brandy), grappa or vodka. Store in a cool, dark place for 40 days.

Filter the liquid and pour it into a bottle. Put 175 g (6 oz) granulated sugar and 125 ml (4 fl oz) water into a saucepan. Bring to the boil, stirring constantly, then remove from the heat. Leave to cool and when it becomes lukewarm, add it to the bottle. Seal the bottle, mix well and store in a cool place.

Placing one 1–2 lemon verbena leaves in the bottle will look attractive.

Apple Fromage Frais

Preparation time: 10 minutes
+ 30 minutes chilling
6 servings

1 kg (2 lb) fromage frais or curd cheese
500 g (1 lb) Dried Apples (see page 134), diced
4 tablespoons clear honey

Place the fromage frais or curd cheese in a large
serving bowl. Add the diced apple and mix well.
Add the honey and stir well to mix. Chill in the
refrigerator for at least 30 minutes before serving.

TIPS: This dish could be served in tall glasses and
eaten with a long spoon.
Leave a small pot of honey available, so that
people can sweeten it to their taste.

Apple Fromage Frais

syrups and alcohol

Prunes in Alcohol

**Preparation time: 15 minutes
+ overnight soaking
No cooking required**

1 kg (2 lb) prunes
500 ml (17 fl oz) weak tea, cooled
1 cinnamon stick
100 g (3½ oz) caster sugar
750 ml (1¼ pints) eau de vie (colourless brandy),
grappa or vodka

Put the prunes in a bowl, pour in the tea and
leave to soak overnight.
Next day, sterilize a preserving jar in a large
saucepan of boiling water for 10 minutes.
Remove the jar and place upside down on a
clean tea towel to drain.
Drain the prunes and pack them into the dry jar.
Add the cinnamon stick and sprinkle in the sugar.
Pour in the eau de vie, grappa or vodka to cover
and seal the jar with an airtight lid.
Store in a cool, dark place for about 3 months
before opening.

Cherries in Alcohol

**Preparation time: 15 minutes
No cooking required**

1 kg (2 lb) ripe, slightly firm cherries,
stalks removed
1 cinnamon stick
150 g (5 oz) caster sugar
750 ml (1¼ pints) eau de vie (colourless brandy),
grappa or vodka

Sterilize a preserving jar in a large saucepan of
boiling water for 10 minutes. Remove and place
upside down on a clean tea towel to drain.
Pack the cherries into the dry jar. Add the
cinnamon stick and sprinkle in the sugar. Pour in
the eau de vie, grappa or vodka to cover and seal
the jar with an airtight lid.
Store in a cool, dark place for about 3 months
before consuming.

Prunes in Alcohol

Old Boy's Jam

Preparation time: this 'jam' is prepared over several months from spring to autumn
Cooking time: 5 minutes

good-quality fruits in season:
strawberries, hulled
apricots, halved and pitted
cherries, stalks removed
raspberries
peaches, pitted and quartered
grapes,
plums, halved and pitted if large
pears, halved and cored.
1 cinnamon stick (optional)
caster sugar
eau de vie (colourless brandy), grappa or vodka

Sterilize a large – at least 3-litre (5 pint) – preserving jar in a large saucepan of boiling water for 10 minutes. Remove and place upside down on a clean tea towel to drain.

Place the first layer of fruit in the base of the dry jar and add the cinnamon stick, if using.

To make the syrup put 150 g (5 oz) sugar into a heavy-based saucepan. Pour in 500 ml (17 fl oz) water and bring to the boil, stirring constantly. Remove the pan from the heat and leave to cool. Pour the syrup over the fruits to cover, then add 250 ml (8 fl oz) eau de vie, grappa or vodka.

Seal the jar with an airtight lid and store in a cool, dark place.

Continue making new layers of different fruits, each time adding syrup to cover and eau de vie, grappa or vodka. Re-seal with an airtight lid and store in a cool, dark place.

When the jar is full, leave for about 3 months before opening.

Old Boy's Jam

Lemon Syrup

Preparation time: 10 minutes + cooling
Cooking time: 15 minutes

1 kg (2 lb) caster sugar
500 ml (17 fl oz) water
1 litre (1¾ pints) lemon juice
grated rind of 1 lemon

Put the sugar into a heavy-based saucepan. Pour in the water and bring to the boil, stirring until the sugar has dissolved. Boil for 2–3 minutes, then remove the pan from the heat and set aside to cool.
Pour the lemon juice into another heavy-based pan and stir in the rind. Add the cooled syrup and heat gently for 5–10 minutes, stirring frequently. Leave to cool, then strain the liquid. Pour into a bottle and seal the top.

Blackcurrant Syrup

Preparation time: 15 minutes + cooling
Cooking time: 5 minutes

1 litre (1¾ pints) blackcurrant juice
875 g (1¾ lb) caster sugar

Pour the blackcurrant juice into a heavy-based saucepan and add the sugar. Bring to the boil, stirring constantly until the sugar has dissolved. Boil for 2–3 minutes, then remove from the heat and leave to cool. Strain the syrup, pour into a bottle and seal the top.

Mint Syrup

Preparation time: 15 minutes + cooling
Cooking time: 10 minutes

4 bunches of mint
1 litre (1¾ pints) water
1 kg (2 lb) caster sugar

Place the mint leaves in a large bowl and pour in boiling water to cover. Cover with clingfilm and leave to infuse overnight.
Next day, strain the liquid into a heavy-based saucepan. Add the sugar and bring to the boil, stirring until the sugar has dissolved. Simmer for about 10 minutes, then remove the pan from the heat and leave to cool. Pour into a bottle and seal the top

Syrups

Peach Wine

Preparation time: 10 minutes
+ 1 month macerating
No cooking required

2 handfuls of peach leaves
1 litre (1¾ pints) sweet white wine
200 ml (7 fl oz) eau de vie (colourless brandy),
grappa or vodka
150 g (5 oz) caster sugar

Place the peach leaves in a large jar. Add the
wine, eau de vie, grappa or vodka and the sugar.
Cover and leave to macerate for about 1 month.
Strain the wine and bottle it.

TIP: Serve well chilled as an aperitif.

Walnut Wine

Preparation time: 10 minutes
+ 1 month macerating
No cooking required

6 fresh walnuts, shelled and quartered
1 litre (1¾ pints) sweet white wine
250 ml (8 fl oz) eau de vie (colourless brandy),
grappa or vodka
150 g (5 oz) caster sugar

Place the walnuts in a large jar. Add the wine,
eau de vie, grappa or vodka and sugar. Cover
and leave to macerate for about 1 month,
stirring occasionally. Strain the wine and bottle it.

TIP: Serve well chilled as an aperitif.
Fresh walnuts, also known as wet walnuts,
are available in the early autumn.

Orange Wine

Preparation time: 10 minutes
+ 8 days macerating
No cooking required

grated rind of 2 oranges
1 litre (1¾ pints) sweet white or rosé wine
200 g (7 oz) caster sugar

Place the orange rind, sugar and wine in a large
bowl. Cover and leave to macerate for 8 days.
Strain the wine and bottle it.

Peach Wine and Walnut Wine

Blackcurrant Kir

Pour a few drops of Blackcurrant Syrup (see page 146) into a glass before adding dry white wine. Serve chilled as an aperitif.

Mint Granita

Fill a large glass with crushed ice and pour a little Mint Syrup (see page 146) over it. Stir and serve with a straw.

Lemon Sorbet with Syrup

A last minute tip: just as you serve a
sorbet, sprinkle it with a few drops of
Lemon Syrup (see page 146).

Peach and Orange Spiced
Fruit Salad

Pour 300 ml (½ pint) Peach Wine (see
page 148) into a pan. Add the juice of
1 orange and a cinnamon stick and
bring to the boil. Remove from the
heat and leave to cool.
Spoon the mixture over fruit salad and
serve well chilled.

Cherry and Rosemary Clafoutis

**Preparation time: 20 minutes
+ 20 minutes standing
Cooking time: 30 minutes
4 servings**

125 g (4 oz) granulated or demerara sugar
1 egg yolk
2 eggs
20 g (¾ oz) plain flour, sifted
25 g (1 oz) ground almonds
200 ml (7 fl oz) milk
100 ml (3½ fl oz) single cream
300 g (10 oz) Cherries in Alcohol (see page 142)
1 rosemary sprig
salt

Whisk together the sugar and egg yolk in a bowl, then whisk in the whole eggs. Fold in the flour, almonds and a pinch of salt and whisk well. Stir in the milk and cream, then set aside in a cool place to rest for 10 minutes.

Meanwhile, arrange the cherries and rosemary in a well-greased ovenproof dish. Whisk the batter again, pour it over the fruit and cook in a preheated oven, 180°C (350°F), Gas Mark 4, for 30 minutes. Leave to stand for about 10 minutes and serve slightly warm.

Cherry and Rosemary Clafoutis

Old Boy's Fresh Fruit Salad

**Preparation time: 15 minutes + 3 hours chilling
No cooking required**

2 oranges, peeled and cut into chunks
2 apples, cored and diced
1 banana, peeled and sliced
1 kiwifruit, peeled and sliced
1 small pineapple, peeled and chopped
1 small mango, peeled, pitted and diced
a few mint leaves
2 tablespoons demerara sugar
200 ml (7 fl oz) liquor from Old Boy's Jam (see page 144)
mint sprigs, to decorate

Place the pieces of fruit in a large bowl, sprinkle the sugar over it, pour on the liquor, and mix gently. Cover with clingfilm and chill for at least 3 hours.
Decorate with mint sprigs and serve well chilled.

TIP: You can add some fruits in alcohol to the fresh fruits, if you wish.

Old Boy's Fresh Fruit Salad

Appendices

Table of Recipes

With thanks to

- *Pasta Luna*, 15 rue Mézières, 75006 Paris, France
- "Airelle" and "Miss Olive"
- Gérard Ciprès for the creation of certain recipes, including the awesome *Cherry and Rosemary Clafoutis*

Bravo to Akiko!

First published by Marabout, an imprint of Hachette-Livre
43 Quai de Grenelle, Paris 75905, Cedex 15, France
© 2002 Marabout (Hachette-Livre)
© Les recettes d'Amandine (text)
© Akiko Ida (photographs)
Under the title Les Recettes d'Amandine, Conserves Maison
All rights reserved

Language translation produced by Translate-A-Book, Oxford

© 2003 English Translation, Octopus Publishing Group Ltd, London
This edition published by Hachette Illustrated UK, Octopus Publishing Group,
2–4 Heron Quays, London, E14 4JP

Proof-reading (French edition) Philippe Rollet
Editing: Chrystel Arnould

ISBN: 1-84430-015-3
Printed by Tien Wah, Singapore